THE ULTIMATE
life organizer

An Interactive Guide to a Simpler, Less Stressful, and More Organized Life

By Lisa Montanaro

PETER PAUPER PRESS, INC.
White Plains, New York

This book is dedicated to my Mom, Carol Montanaro,
who always stressed the importance of keeping a clean and organized home,
and managed to do so with warmth and love.
Her unwavering love and support made me the woman I am today.
She was the best mother and friend a daughter could have asked for.

Acknowledgments

I wish to gratefully acknowledge my editor at Peter Pauper Press, Barbara Paulding,
for her willingness to answer my questions and for her encouraging tone
throughout this project. You made my first official book publishing
experience a pleasure and I thank you for it!

Special thanks to my father, Joseph Montanaro, who makes Felix Unger look disorganized!
A big thank you to my sister-in-law, Elizabeth Hulsebosch, for guiding me through my first publishing
deal. To my soul sister and friend, Tracy Stroh, who was my first organizing client, thanks for starting
me down the path to professional organizing many years ago. And to my stepfather,
John Paradise, thanks for your never ending support of this project, and of all my endeavors.

My deep gratitude to the hundreds of clients I've been privileged to work with in
my professional organizing career. Working with you has provided me with valuable lessons
and improved my professional skills. Your willingness to trust me with your organizing projects,
big and small, has made this an amazing and worthwhile journey.

And, finally, a big thank you to my husband, Sean Hulsebosch. Without your ongoing support,
sense of humor, and love, I would never have finished this book while running a thriving business
and grieving the loss of my beloved mother. You truly embody the word "partner" in every way.

Designed by Heather Zschock

Visit us at www.peterpauper.com

THE ULTIMATE
life organizer

*An Interactive Guide to a Simpler,
Less Stressful, and More Organized Life*

contents

introduction

Organizing is what you do before you do something, so that when you do it, it is not all mixed up.

A. A. MILNE

welcome!

An organized life. Sounds good, doesn't it? But, what exactly does it mean to live an organized life? The answer is, "It depends." It depends on your definition of organized. My definition is when you can easily find the things you need, love, and want, and your life functions smoothly.

You either picked up this book on your own, or received it as a gift. Chances are you are interested in getting more organized. Maybe you have to move papers in order to eat at the dining room table. Perhaps you are often late for work because you can't find your keys in the morning. Or worse, you are late paying bills because you don't have a simple bill-paying system and constantly get stuck with late fees. Sound familiar? If so, this book is for you!

Getting the Most from this Book

Think of this book as your companion as you work to better organize your life, home, and work environments. Here is all the guidance you need to walk the path to an organized life. This book also serves as the place where you write down your organizing challenges, goals, and triumphs along the way. Designed so that each chapter can stand alone, this book allows you to go out of order (yes, in an organizing book!), or you can read it straight through in order to get a "big picture" overview. As your personal organizing coach, I've included lots of tools—such as checklists, charts, exercises, and places to journal—to make the process fun and easy-to-follow.

The journal pages provide a safe haven to work through your desires, dreams, obstacles, challenges, and goals. Journaling is a great way to dialogue with yourself, and often leads to powerful breakthroughs. Something magical happens when you put words down on paper. Words are powerful in and of themselves. But writing down words is even more powerful! I received my first journal as a gift when I was eight years old. I have filled countless journals since then, and journaling remains vitally important to me up until this day. So think of the journal entries as a gift to yourself.

To get the most from this book, I recommend you follow some simple "rules." (Of course there are rules in an organizing book! Did you think I'd let you off that easy?)

1. **Take a quick peek at the entire book, either through the Table of Contents or by skimming the chapters.** This will give you an idea of what is covered, and will whet your appetite for sections that particularly appeal to you.

2. **Do the exercises!** You are not being graded. There are no wrong answers. But, your answers will reveal a lot. The exercises are designed to be thought provoking, and help you assess where you are and how far you need to go in order to live an organized life. Your answers will help you figure out which areas of your home, work, and life need the most attention, which possessions are truly meaningful to you, and what you are ready to let go of during the organizing process.

3. **Go slowly.** The process presented in this book is meant to be worked through over time. Don't rush through, fail miserably, then use that as an excuse to stop making progress. Take it one step at a time. Small steps can make a big difference and lead to significant and lasting change. The entire book will take some people a few days, while others may spend months or even years going through the process. Most people will start to see results pretty quickly, however. For the average space, even a few hours of organizing can make a difference. But to see real lasting results, commit yourself to devoting a few hours per week over a longer period of time. This is not a race! Go at your own pace.

4. **Celebrate your success, no matter how small.** As with any behavior modification program, you will want to reward yourself along the way for reaching goals. Success builds momentum, and will inspire you to keep going.

CHAPTER 1:
the inner game of being organized

Reduce the complexity of life by eliminating the needless wants of life, and the labors of life reduce themselves.

EDWIN WAY TEALE

People who say they have no time to get organized are usually the very ones who need it the most. They are losing time searching for items they don't know how to find, and are not getting rid of the clutter that takes up precious real estate in their physical environments and their minds.

Why is living an organized life so important? Let's examine some of the benefits. Being organized positively affects your time, money, health, space, reputation, and relationships. Organized people save time (time lost to searching for missing items), save money (not buying duplicates anymore as they know what they have, avoiding late fees by paying bills on time, etc.), have lower stress, and are able to focus on what they really want to accomplish, whether that is work related, self time, or family time.

Getting organized is about decluttering your life, clearing out the unnecessary items in every area—from your desktop and files, to your calendar and computer—then implementing systems that keep only the most loved and useful stuff in its place. Being organized has less to do with the way an environment looks than how effectively it functions. The goal is not just to be organized, but for your life, home, and office to run more smoothly. One of the best benefits of being organized is that when life throws you a curve ball, you can hit it and get on base. You can't avoid the curve ball, but being organized helps you deal with it better by having systems in place to fall back on.

One cannot discover new oceans unless he has the courage to lose sight of the shore.

ANDRE GIDE

How Disorganized Are We? The Sobering Reality

By all accounts, people today are more disorganized than ever. And yet, we are more advanced, wealthy, and educated than ever as well. Then why are we so disorganized? Well, for starters, we have more stuff! We are also pressed for time, as society gets more and more busy. However, all of our material possessions and busyness has not led to achieving peak productivity. Quite the opposite. It has caused serious disorganization. For example, *USA Today* reports that Americans collectively waste nine million hours every day looking for misplaced items.

I tell you this not to depress you, but to let you know that you are not alone! Many high functioning, intelligent people are disorganized. They are just working too hard to compensate for their disorganization. Can you learn to be better organized? Yes! Organizing is a skill that can be learned, but unfortunately it is not taught in school. This book provides the perspective, expert advice, and strategies you need to get organized, simply and effectively. Your life will feel, and be, more balanced.

What Is Clutter?

What is clutter? The answer depends on whom you ask. For many disorganized people, nothing is clutter (a definition that sometimes leads in the extreme to hoarding). For others, clutter is anything that piles up above and beyond their normal possessions. I like to say that clutter is like a weed in a garden. It is something that doesn't belong. Either you did not plant it, it got carried along to a new location where it shouldn't be, or it has outgrown its space. It can even be a plant or flower that you planted and loved at one time, but now decide no longer belongs. In other words, *clutter is anything that you don't love, want, need, or use.*

Regardless of whether the clutter is physical or mental, it is caused by a combination of forces that create disorganization. Your role is to assess why the clutter is in your home, office, and life and then prepare to get rid of it. The best motivation for clearing clutter is not to focus on the time and energy needed to sort your stuff, but to ask yourself, "What am I creating space for?"

The only way you can effectively declutter is to eliminate the constant mantra of "But I might need that someday." Ask yourself: What's the worst thing that can happen if I donate, recycle, or toss the item? If you can live with the answer, get rid of it! The key to dealing with clutter is being able to assess your needs and motives in order to find out why you are keeping your clutter. Once you understand your motives, you can eliminate clutter for good—and greatly improve your sense of inner well-being.

Disorganization—Getting to the Root of the Problem

There are many reasons why people get disorganized. But first, let's go back to the beginning—your childhood. Were you ever taught organizing skills?

Many people find themselves disorganized due to their upbringing. Perhaps your parents did not model organized behavior. Maybe you grew up in a disorganized environment and just accepted it as a way of life. In addition, maybe you weren't lucky enough to have someone pull you aside and show you organizing principles, like a teacher or other adult role model in your life. To top it off, most schools do not teach organizing skills, so you probably did not have the opportunity to take a class on organizing (a fact that the National Association of Professional Organizers is trying to change through its NAPO in the Schools Program).

On the flip side, maybe you had an ultra-organized parent who did everything for you, so you never learned organizing principles yourself. Instead of transferring organizing skills to you, your parent did it all, depriving you of the opportunity to learn behavior that would serve you well throughout your life. If this is the case, don't get bogged down in blame. Learn the skills now! It is never too late to get organized.

Take a moment to write your thoughts about how your early life has affected your organizational style (or lack thereof!).

Common Reasons for Disorganization

Take a look at some of the common reasons for disorganization below and check the ones that reflect your situation.

Space-Based Issues

☐ Items have no "home"

☐ Inconvenient or insufficient storage space

External Barriers

☐ Uncooperative partners at home or at the office

☐ Downsizing at work, creating more work for those still employed

☐ The speed of life

☐ Information overload, especially in the area of technology gadgets, which were invented to improve our productivity but can be distracting, thus causing disorganization.

☐ Transitional disorganization—There are times when being organized will be more challenging than others. When life is in transition, it often causes disorganization. For example, the holiday season is often chaotic for many, even though it is supposed to be joyful. Certain life transitions, such as moving, starting school, searching for a new job, becoming an empty nester, or retiring, bring their own challenges and can cause temporary disorganization. Even happy occasions, such as marrying, getting a promotion at work, having a baby, or planning a vacation, can throw the most organized people off balance.

Internal Barriers

☐ Delayed decisions

☐ Unclear goals and priorities

☐ Consumerism—The need for abundance (the drive to buy)

☐ Perfectionism—The need for perfection

The 5 Fears:

☐ Fear of success/fear of failure (two sides of the same coin)

☐ Fear of losing creativity if things are orderly

☐ Fear of change/disruption of status quo

☐ Fear of completion

☐ Fear of downtime/need for distraction

☐ Disliking your physical space

☐ Sentimental attachment to physical possessions (e.g., unwanted gifts, saving for later, and mementos)

☐ Keeping items out of guilt

Physical Limitations

☐ Physical disability

☐ Health problems

Mental Health Issues

☐ Chronic Disorganization (CD)—According to the National Study Group on Chronic Disorganization (www.NSGCD.org), chronic disorganization is defined as "having a past history of disorganization in which self-help efforts to change have failed, an undermining of current quality of life due to disorganization, and the expectation of future disorganization."

☐ Attention Deficit/Hyperactivity Disorder (ADD/ADHD)—As defined by the Mayo Clinic, adult attention-deficit/hyperactivity disorder (adult ADHD) is a "mental health condition that causes inattention, hyperactivity and impulsive behavior." Adult ADHD symptoms can lead to a number of problems, including unstable relationships, poor work or school performance, low self-esteem, and the inability to develop and maintain organizing systems.

☐ Hoarding—There is no clear definition of compulsive hoarding in accepted diagnostic references, but medical experts Randy O. Frost and Tamara L. Hartl identify three characteristics: "(1) the acquisition of, and failure to discard a large number of possessions that appear to be useless or of limited value; (2) living spaces sufficiently cluttered so as to preclude activities for which those spaces were designed; and (3) significant distress or impairment in functioning caused by the hoarding."

Get Organized Self-Assessment

Which of the reasons for disorganization in the previous exercise did you identify with?

Why did things get this way? (Use the list of common reasons for disorganization to help you identify the "why.")

What is your purpose or what are your goals for wanting to get better organized?

What are your strengths and weaknesses?

Are there areas of your home, office, or life that are already organized? Did you set up those organizing systems? How?

Have you tried to get organized in the past and were unable to? In what areas of your home, office, or life? Do you know why you were unable to succeed?

What is your disorganization preventing you from having in your life or work?

Take a moment to write your thoughts about your organizational self-assessment.

Are You Ready to Get Organized?

How do you know if you need a new organizing system? Ask yourself if the current system is really working. Unless your current system is truly effective most of the time, start from scratch and set up a system that truly works! Ask yourself how frustrated you are with your physical surroundings, your inability to manage time, and the clutter in your life. If something is really bothering you, chances are you'll know it!

What Is the Best Way to Get Organized?

While there are general organizing principles, there is no "cookie cutter" solution to getting organized. Don't let that depress you. Quite the contrary, it should give you hope! For an organizing system to stick, it must be built around your personality type, work style, physical environment, and needs and goals, so be sure to tailor everything in this book to make it work for you. Yes, you should use the general organizing principles on pages 23–27, but always in a way that is personal and authentic to you.

You have your own particular organizing style, even if you don't know exactly what it is! If you are familiar with the four learning styles, start there. They are visual (learn by seeing), auditory (learn by hearing/listening), kinesthetic (learn by doing), and tactile (learn by touching).

There is an ever-increasing number of products and services designed to help a person get organized. First, however, you must determine the areas in which you want to improve in order to identify your organizing goals. These might be filing, clutter control, time management, maximization of storage space, or juggling projects and priorities.

Organizing ADD

If you are overwhelmed, just thinking about getting organized may cause you to suffer from what I've termed "Organizing ADD." That is when you have so many pockets of clutter and disorganization in your life that it's overwhelming, making it difficult to begin the process. If this accurately describes you, fear not! Take a deep breath, grab a glass of water, and fill out the chart on the pages that follow. It will help you identify organizing obstacles and start to formulate a plan of action.

Walk around your home and your office. Also scrutinize your calendar, computer, and e-mail inbox. Take notes in the space provided. If you are not quite ready to put pen to paper, at least start by using a "virtual clipboard" where you take stock mentally. Start to identify the clutter that you can get rid of during the organizing process.

Take Stock of Clutter

What categories of clutter do you have in each area? Are they in designated places?

	Mudroom/ Entryway	Kitchen	Den/ Playrooms	Living Room
Mail/Papers				
School papers/ Kids' artwork				
Clothing				
Toys				
Books				
Magazines & Newspapers				

Dining Room	Master Bedroom	Kids' Rooms/ Extra Bedrooms	Office	Other

Reflect on the results of taking stock of your clutter on the preceding pages. Think about what is true for you, and answer the following:

Which categories include the most clutter?

Do you love these items? Which ones?

Do you need these items? Which ones?

Which items do you use often?

Which items would you not miss if they went away?

What would you like to replace them with, if anything?

What areas of your house and office need priority attention?

Take a moment to write your thoughts about your results, above.

The Joy of the Organizing Journey

Focus on the journey, not the destination. Joy is found not in finishing an activity, but in doing it.

GREG ANDERSON

Many people cringe at the prospect of doing the actual physical organizing process. Yes, I know it doesn't seem like fun. But not only will it be worth it in the long run, you may be surprised that you enjoy the journey. Some people experience the euphoria of letting go and feel lighter, happier, and gain a sense of freedom even after their first organizing session. Once you start exercising your organizing muscles, you experience the positive benefits, and gain momentum. This makes each successive step in the process easier.

Always keep in mind that as you release clutter of any kind, you are freeing up precious space for new (and hopefully better!) items and opportunities to come into your life (or maybe just open space so that you have room to breathe). From an energy standpoint, many cultures believe that until the clutter is cleared, beauty cannot flow in. Regardless of what you believe, I have seen the results hundreds of times. When people clear clutter and get organized, even in some subtle ways, positive change occurs. So try to enjoy the journey itself, and let the power of the process unfold naturally and work its magic.

Change Is the Name of the Game

Are you ready to change? Be bold and be broad. Getting organized requires that you think about what you really want in your life, and that you be willing to let go of some things in order to make room for others.

In order to get organized, you have to be willing to make changes in your systems and the way you are doing things (or not doing things), and you have to be prepared to act—to put the general organizing principles (see pages 23–27) in place. It took you a long time to get disorganized, so be prepared to put in the time to make or break habits—psychologists say it takes about 18 days to do so.

Remember that change is a process, not an event. Don't try to change everything at once. Pick one area of your life that needs changing most and focus on it first. And when you create a new organizational system, keep it simple. If it's too complicated, you won't stick to it.

Overcoming Temporary Organizing Paralysis

As you start the organizing journey, you may suffer from what I like to call, Temporary Organizing Paralysis. This is when you start organizing, freeze up, stare at all of the stuff and think, "Where do I begin? What am I going to do with all of this stuff?"

Realize that it will get worse before it gets better if you are in the middle of an organizing project. The stuff will be out of the drawers, files, closets, etc. Come up with a staging area to sort the stuff, so it is not in the way. That will help keep your stress level down. Also, identify early on who and where to donate items: friends and family, thrift shops, places of worship, domestic violence shelters, homeless shelters, etc. There are many willing homes for used stuff. Adopting a charity or a needy family makes getting rid of your clutter a whole lot easier.

Often, there is a domino effect of being disorganized. You may need to start somewhere else in order to clear space first before you can work on a particular organizing project. For example, let's say you have paper all over your dining room table (a common clutter catcher spot!). You would think of starting on the dining room table. But the real problem is your home office. You haven't cleared out the paper bins and filing drawers in so long that you can't bring any new paper into that room. Thus, you started piling it on the table. Therefore, you need to start in the home office, clear clutter, make room, and then move to the dining room table. So, give some thought to the order of your organizing projects and how one may affect another. Of course, if you desperately need or want your dining room table back before your home office is organized, you can temporarily box up the papers on the table and move them to a staging area and work there while getting organized. If you have the space to create "organizing central," then go ahead and do it. Get some boxes, bins, a folding table, and go to town!

Staying Motivated

In order to stay motivated while organizing, post your list of goals (see page 22) in a conspicuous place, especially if you are a visual person. Before and after photos also help many people get and stay motivated. Consider playing some upbeat music to keep you alert, or relaxing music if you are easily distracted. If you dread organizing alone, work with your spouse or a friend, involve your kids, or go pro and hire a professional organizer. (Visit the Web site of the National Association of Professional Organizers at www.NAPO.net to find an organizer near you.) And, don't forget to reward yourself along the way as you would with any other behavior modification program.

Getting organized is about making progress, not achieving perfection. Don't be daunted by the prospect of getting organized. Just take it one step at a time. You'll have more chance of success if you break the overall project into manageable tasks, tackling a little bit at a time. The key is to get started and stay focused. You can do it!

Set Your Organizing Goals

List your organizing goals here. There are no "right" goals when it comes to organizing. Whatever comes to mind when you ask yourself why you want to get better organized is the right answer. Here are a few common goals to help stimulate your goal setting.

- Improve quality of life.
- Be able to find things when I need them.
- Save time.
- Save money.
- Improve my relationship with my spouse.
- Model good behavior for my kids.

Now list your goals below.

General Organizing Principles

Drum roll, please. Here they are—tips, tricks, and tools to get you started on your organizing journey to the Land of Being Able to Find Things!

Think inside the box. Start thinking of all of your spaces as finite, with only a certain amount of room to fill. This will limit your perception of space to one closer to reality and will force you to stay within the box of space provided. **Set up organizing rotation systems.** Here are a few to consider:

- **Clothes**—If you live in a climate that experiences the change of seasons, you probably already rotate your clothes. This involves switching your wardrobe by putting away clothes from one season into storage and taking out the clothes for the upcoming season. This is one of the most common organizing rotation systems and one that many people take for granted and do naturally.

- **Toys**—If your children have too many toys but are not ready to donate some just yet, you can put select toys in storage, and periodically take them out and switch them with the current toys. Some people refer to this as the toy library system where their kids can go and "check out" toys from the toy library, bringing back another toy to store in its place. That way, the toys that are displayed in the house stay at a manageable level.

- **Home Décor**—People naturally keep Christmas and other holiday decorations in storage throughout the year and take them out only during the relevant season. You can take this a step further and put many of your home décor items in rotation: linens, window treatments, mementos, and collections, etc. This way, you can keep and display more of the things you love, and match the décor to your mood or the season.

Choose "homes" for your possessions. If clutter is delayed decisions, then make each decision easier by having a ready-made place for every possession that crosses your path. Everything in its place equals harmony. Store like items together in a home that makes sense to you. (And, no, throwing clothes in the same pile on your treadmill that you haven't used in months does not count as an appropriate home!)

Ideas for implementing:

Categorize. Group like items together according to how you use them and set up zones for maximizing time and efficiency. For example, coffee making station, gift-wrap center, bill paying center. This is often described as the Kindergarten Room Principle—having a "zone" for every project.

Ideas for implementing:

Set up a "launching or landing" pad for frequently used items. Think of everything you need to launch your day in the morning, and everything you need to land when you get home in the evening.

Ideas for implementing:

Think vertical when looking for storage space. Most people tend to store items on the horizontal plane between their shoulders and knees for easy access. But if you have already decluttered and are truly running out of space, use "kick space" and "air space." Bare walls, behind the door, and above cabinets are often sorely underutilized. And also think down and under—under the bed, the bottom of closets, etc.

Ideas for implementing:

Create organizing systems to be used by many people with all users in mind. Would you love to delegate more but find it difficult because no one but you would be able to find anything? If you're the only person who knows where anything is, you're making it harder on yourself! Develop simple organizing systems with homes for items that are easy to find so that others can help you out. Consider holding a family meeting to discuss multi-user systems and get everyone involved and invested in the outcome. Spend time brainstorming how each person plans to use the system, and create a compromise that makes the most sense.

Ideas for implementing:

If you don't love it, use it often, or need it, then toss (or donate) it! Moving around, or even organizing, things you should just get rid of ends up being a long-term game of musical clutter! Come up with a value system for determining what to keep and what to purge. Throw out or donate the things that no longer serve you regardless of what you paid for them or whether they are "perfectly good." If you don't use it or love it, it is not "perfectly good" for you! Sometimes clients will hoard three coffee makers, for example, just in case one breaks. But the fact is, by the time it breaks, a better one will be on the market. Think about who you know that might benefit from having something you don't really use, and then give it away.

Ideas for implementing:

Give prized possessions and things that you love a place of honor. Let the cream rise to the top. Remember, if everything is important, then nothing is important. A diamond in the rough is a lot more special than a bunch of rocks!

Ideas for implementing:

Stop acquiring! Limit what you buy in the first place. The more you have, the more you have to manage. If you buy it, you have to clean it, store it, and sometimes insure it, and there's a limit to what one person can do. Ask if each item is worth inviting into your life. Think about that before you shop.

Ideas for implementing:

Donate Your Castaway Items

You can probably think of many items in your home to donate. Start looking around, with an eye toward identifying items to donate. Make a list, gather those items, and take them to a homeless shelter, domestic violence safe home, religious institution, thrift shop, or any other place that accepts donations. If you want to be able to deduct those donated items from your taxes, be sure to itemize your donations in writing, estimate their worth, and get a receipt. There is software that itemizes donations, or you can search online and use thrift shop values, which are commonly acceptable.

List items to donate here:

There you have it—the Inner Game of Being Organized. If you can conquer your barriers internally, and start to focus externally on what you love, use often, and need, the decluttering will be a whole lot easier. As you write down your thoughts in the journal pages that follow, think about this: "What do I own, and what owns me? How do I feel getting rid of things?" Remember to focus on what you are making space for, figuratively and literally. Congratulations. You are on your way!

Notes

Perfection is achieved, not when there is nothing more to add, but when there is nothing left to take away.

ANTOINE DE SAINT-EXUPÉRY

CHAPTER 2:
time management

The passage of time drives you crazy when you know perfectly well you're not using it right.

BARBARA SHER

Almost everyone thinks they need to improve their time management skills. The oft-repeated phrase, "time management," is itself an oxymoron. You can't manage time, only what you choose to do with it. I often tell my clients that if I could invent a time machine and give them all a 25th hour in the day, I would. But until that amazing feat occurs, we are all left on an even playing field.

People are not overwhelmed with time itself, but with what they fill that time with—all of the tasks and responsibilities that make up their busy schedules. That overwhelmed feeling is due to a lack of control over the passing of time. And it's true: No matter how hard you try, you cannot control the passing of time.

Your Relationship with Time

Much of what has been written about time management focuses on using tips, tricks, and tools to get more things done. The problem with that approach is that there will always be more tasks to be done. We have become a culture of fast-paced, multi-tasking doers. And that may work for some. In fact, some of you may be eager to get to the time management strategies. Be patient—we will get to them, I promise!

But first, let's bring in the part that is not about getting things done, but about enjoying your life—relaxation, hobbies, family time, and self time. You can't ignore your relationship with time. We must cover that first in order to then put the time management tools in proper context.

Let's start by dispelling a common myth: the phrase "Time is money." As Benjamin Franklin once pointed out, time isn't money—time is life itself: "Dost thou love life? Then do not squander time, for that is the stuff life is made of."

No amount of money in the world can buy a minute or an hour. I hope you can always manage to make another dollar in your lifetime. But the moment that just passed while you were reading this sentence will never happen again. Thus, don't belittle time by equating it with money. Put time in its proper place, which should be a place of honor. But also realize that time is forgiving, as you get to start over each day with a chance to live life to the fullest and use all 24 hours in the best way possible. So let the connection between time and life itself be the impetus you need for managing your time better.

Managing time is really about managing yourself and making choices that are in alignment with your goals. Try to get a glimpse of what it would be like to live your life in a way that is more consistent with your goals, and honors you and the people in your life more fully. You make powerful choices on a daily basis. Every choice you make about how to spend your time is a conscious choice not to spend it doing something else.

Be honest with yourself. What do you want from your time? What is your motivation for wanting to manage your time better? Be open to challenging yourself and some typical time management thinking. Try on some time management techniques. Not all techniques will work for everyone, so pay attention to the strategies that particularly appeal to you. Be ready for any breakthroughs that may occur.

Notes:

Time Management Self-Assessment

This exercise will help you identify your time management challenges and goals.

If I could spend time doing anything I wanted, it would be

I find myself wishing every day that I had made time for this activity:

One task or activity that I do make time for every day is

I am always late for this activity:

I am always on time for this activity:

I lose all track of time when doing this activity:

I always procrastinate when I have to do this activity:

If there was another hour in the day, I would spend it

If there was less time in the day, I would cut out

If I could work only three days per week, I would

When I am really busy and pressed for time, the first task or activity I cut out or say "no" to is

If I had all the time I needed, how would my life be different?

If this book helps me "save" time, what will I do with the time I save?

What do my responses to the exercise above tell me?

Notes

Create a Time Journal

Human beings, by changing the inner attitudes of their minds, can change the outer aspects of their lives.

WILLIAM JAMES

Consider making a "time journal" of your life for a week. Just like people who are on a weight loss program will keep a food journal and those on a budget will track finances, you will write down all of your tasks for a week. The time journal is a powerful tool for discovering how long things take you and what you are spending your time on. You will be surprised at how much you underestimate the time it takes to do things you normally do, and overestimate the things you are not as familiar with and don't do as often.

Pick a typical week so that you get a true snapshot of your life. At the end of the week, tally up time by categories or activity type. For example, you can create categories such as getting ready in the morning, commuting to work, household chores, errands, exercise, family time, work, "me" time, etc. You can be as detailed or broad as you want. However, if you want to track a particular activity, for example, how long you spend on e-mail, then you must track that activity in a detailed manner. Remember, knowledge is power! Be mindful as well of the amount of sleep you're getting. Most people require at least seven hours of sleep a night for physical and emotional health and to perform at peak productivity.

A few guidelines:

- Do not judge yourself as you are tracking time in your time journal. Save the assessment for later.

- You do not need to get fancy. Use the calendar on the pages that follow (you can copy it if you want to track more than one week), or use your own online calendar system, daily planner, or smart phone's calendar application. If you want to use time tracking software, go right ahead. Just don't let the project itself take too much time or effort. If so, you will dread doing it, or worse, use the time journal as a distraction from the bigger project, which is using it to improve your time management skills.

- If you are a strong visual learner, you may consider color-coding by category. It is a handy way to look back at the end of the week and get a visual snapshot of each category.

My Time Journal

Fill in tasks and activities, tracking how much time spent on them daily over the course of a week. Use the chart on page 40 to tally them up by category for the week.

	Sunday	Monday	Tuesday
7AM			
8AM			
9AM			
10AM			
11AM			
12PM			
1PM			
2PM			
3PM			
4PM			
5PM			
6PM			
7PM			
8PM			
9PM			
10PM			
11PM			

Wednesday	Thursday	Friday	Saturday

Add up time you've spent in the categories you tracked in your Time Journal on the previous pages, and record them below.

Tasks and Activites Tracked	Time Spent Daily	Time Spent Weekly
Working		
Family time		
Leisure or "me" time		
Exercise		

Consider if the ratios reflect your values. If not, identify where and how adjustments could be made. Are there activities important to you that you spend little or no time on?

A time journal is a great way to keep life in balance. If you start feeling that you are losing control of your time, you can revisit your time journal or create a fresh one. Compare how you've been spending your time with how you would spend it if you were doing what is most important to you, and living your life in alignment with your goals. If there are glaring discrepancies, you have your first clue about things you need to change to make your life more balanced and satisfying.

Time Management Techniques

Now that you've completed your time journal and learned about the way you view and use time, get ready to make some changes to your time management techniques. You need techniques to put your plans into action so that you can avoid, to the extent possible, the time crunches that can come between you and your best life.

It is the curse of the modern world. Too much to do and too little time to do it.

Jeremy Laurance

Opportunity Overload

In the 21st century, we are experiencing opportunity overload. We have never been busier, and yet most people say they crave a simpler, less harried existence. The problem is that most people spend a lot of time thinking about how much or how little time they have, but not planning or managing their time. Yet, preparing and planning for the future is the most critical step to time management. If your schedule is stuffed with too many tasks and activities, you will experience opportunity overload. At that point, you need to unclog your calendar.

Unclog Your Calendar

Start by realizing that each person has a certain capacity for getting things done based on time, energy, and the reality of life. Identify tasks on your calendar, agenda, or to-do list that you don't really need to do and let them go. You can revisit them again on another day, or delete them altogether. If you cram every moment of your life with activity, you will wind up late for something. You will also feel stressed out, and not have time for transitions and spontaneous moments. Leave some wiggle room in that schedule!

Here are some tips for unclogging your calendar.

Keep Just One Calendar

- Keep just one calendar or planner to have a place to write all appointments. It doesn't matter what kind it is. Just be sure it is only one. Why? Because as soon as you add more than one calendar to the mix, you create an opportunity for conflicting appointments.

Paper, Electronic, or Both?

- Visual people tend to do better with paper calendars, which allow them to see time and lists in a layout rather than as individual items. Tactile people like pen to paper and enjoy writing, color coordinating by category, and being creative. If this matches your style, by all means, stay with a paper system, but make it work for you, and realize its limitations.

- The disadvantages to a paper calendar/planner in this day and age are many. A paper calendar or planner can be lost and there is no back-up. Paper calendars also can be bulky to carry around and have a limited and finite amount of space. Electronic calendar/planner devices are small, easy to carry, allow you to set alarms and issue reminders, store an amazing amount of information in a small space, and are backed up in case of theft or loss.

- If your company or family uses an electronic calendar system, it makes sense to synch with that same system. If you like the visual layout of a paper calendar, you can always print out a week or month at a time, but remember that you then have to update the electronic version every time you add in an appointment on the paper printout.

Create a Master Calendar

- A master calendar is helpful for facilitating communication in a family (or office) environment. Even in today's technologically advanced world, an old-fashioned wall calendar is a great organizing tool for most busy families. Centralize the information so that everyone's activities for the month can be seen at a glance. Any appointment of your spouse's that will affect you or the children goes on it, and vice versa. You can even consider color-coding based on person or activity.

- Or, go high tech and synchronize electronic calendars so that family members (or staff, if using a master calendar at work) can check each other's schedules and invite each other to appointments and meetings without having to take the time to call. Give access to all family members at home (and to all individuals in the workplace that you frequently need to meet with regularly). Consider an online calendar for the entire family. It is free, easy to use, can be color-coded for each member of the family, and can be maintained by teens on their own.

Love (and Learn) the One You're With

- If you use an electronic calendar system of any kind, learn how to use it! Many people have all of the gadgets with tons of bells and whistles, but don't know how to use them and maximize their power. Read the manuals, watch the tutorials, play the instructional DVDs they come with, and harness their productivity power!

Just Say "No"

- Being chronically overbooked is likely to make you cranky and increase your stress level. Practice the art of saying "no," and don't overschedule your calendar!

- Eliminate one or two social activities that you'd really rather not do and give yourself the gift of some free time. Get rid of two or three projects that sounded like a good idea at the time, but have been collecting dust for the last several months. Once you start exercising your "no" muscles, it will get easier, I promise.

- How to phrase your NO answer, stand firm, but not hurt feelings:
    - "I'd love to, but I can't."
    - "If I take this on, I will not do justice to the project."
    - "You will not be getting my best work and I don't like to give anything less than 100 percent."

Learn the Art of Stalling Your Response

- When asked to do something that would add to your schedule, stall first so you can gather your thoughts before you reply. Ask yourself if you can fit this activity into your schedule, if you want to do it, and if you are the best person to do it. Many times we quickly respond "yes" when we need more time to formulate our answer and a plan!

- The next time you are confronted with anything, from a party invitation to a request for bake sale goodies, curb that automatic yes response and ask: "Will I look forward to this or dread it?" If it's the latter, politely (but firmly) decline!

- Be careful you are not delaying the inevitable. Don't say, "maybe," "we'll see," or "not this time," if you really want to say "no." They will ask you again. If you mean "no," say it!

Break Time Down

- Don't take on too much at one time. Break up large jobs into smaller, more manageable tasks and only focus on each task as a small step in the process. Also, assume projects will take longer than expected and plan accordingly.

- Buffer your schedule with transition time between activities and appointments. If you wind up not needing the transition time (there was no traffic, you found a parking space easily, there were no interruptions, etc.), then consider it a bonus! You will have some "found time," which is so rare in most schedules these days. Enjoy it.

Pass the Buck

- When considering a task or activity on your agenda, think about whether someone else can do it. Yes, this is known as delegating, and it is the most psychological aspect of time and project management as it involves issues of trust and control. It also takes time in the short term to explain a task or assignment, or even perhaps train someone how to do it. But it almost always saves time in the long run, so give delegation some serious attention.

- Delegation may also involve a cost (for example, hiring a cleaning service). If you can use that time to make more money in your business/career, it may be worth it from a cost-benefit analysis standpoint. However, it also may be worth it if it frees you up to focus on more important tasks, or just to spend the time doing things you hardly ever get to do.

- You can delegate tasks and activities to an expert, an equal, or a beginner. Assess whether someone else can do the activity or task better than you, faster than you, or well enough. To gain more time in your schedule, maybe well enough is good enough!

Review the preceding tips for unclogging your calendar, and take note of which ones you will implement and how.

To-Do Lists: You Gotta Keep 'em Separated

To-do lists. Just the name of them sounds exhausting. They have become the thorn in many people's sides. Whether they are written in long form on paper, or maintained electronically on a computer or handheld device, they cause much stress.

And here's one reason why. Most people unknowingly combine their master to-do list and daily to-do list together. This one act causes the list to become lengthy and overwhelming, which in turn almost guarantees failure. The person with this massive all-in-one to-do list will either abort the list altogether, or try desperately to get tasks done, all the while feeling inadequate and like a failure due to his or her inability to accomplish the items on the list.

What to do? (Yes, pun intended!) Keep 'em separated!

Create a master to-do list and a separate daily to-do list. The master list includes tasks you plan to and want to get to, but cannot accomplish in one day, similar to a project list. Your daily list is made up only of the tasks you intend to do, and can realistically accomplish, in one day, which is usually only about three to five items. The daily list puts your master list into action on a daily basis. That way, you get the satisfaction of actually crossing off your daily to-dos, but have a more comprehensive list so you don't forget tasks you need to tend to at some point later on.

Here's an example. You need to do a home renovation project, like paint your basement. Your master to-do list reads: paint basement. But the daily to-do list will break down that master item into several separate entries over a longer period of time.

- **Monday:** Choose paint color.
- **Tuesday:** Call three painters for estimates. (This is called delegating.)
- **Wednesday:** Clear furniture from area to be painted.
- **Thursday:** Buy paint.

Get the picture? The master to-do list names the project and the daily to-do list breaks out the action steps in a manageable, reasonable, and realistic manner in order to accomplish that project. This way, the tasks actually get done. And isn't that what a to-do list is supposed to be for anyway?

Don't forget to add a time element to your daily to-do list. This is one of the most important, but frequently overlooked, parts of time management. You are in a better position to determine whether you can manage the task and fit it into your daily schedule if you know how long it takes to accomplish. Then you don't think, "What can I start?" but rather, "What can I finish?" Add up your to-do items for the day and see how many hours they will take. And don't forget to add in a buffer before and after tasks. Even the most realistic time frames need a cushion to account for interruptions and the unexpected.

Create a Master To-Do List
and a Daily To-Do List

Nothing is so fatiguing as the eternal hanging on of an uncompleted task.

WILLIAM JAMES

Gather all of the post-it notes, scraps of paper, memos, and lists that you have lying around your home and office, and in your purse, wallet, car, and pockets (not to mention in your computer or smart phone!). Group tasks and activities into a Master To-Do List by category (see pages 48–49), and then pull out only a reasonable amount of tasks to complete in a day in order to create your Daily To-Do List (opposite) for the first day that you begin this new to-do list system. (You may copy these forms for future use as well.) The Master To-Do List can be broken down by category (personal, work, home renovation, kids, etc.), by type of task or activity (to call, to pay, to e-mail, etc.), or by deadline (this week, next week, next month, in three months, in six months, in one year, etc.). There is no "right" way to set up a Master To-Do List. Just make sure all of the tasks and activities are in one place!

Copy these fill-in lists for your convenience.

Daily To-Do List, Week of:

Monday	Tuesday	Wednesday	Thursday	Friday	Weekend

Master To-Do List:

	Personal	Work	Home	Family
Task				
Task				
Task				
Task				
Task				
Task				
Task				
Task				

Other	Other	Other	Other	Target Date	Com- pleted

Create a Master Household Chores List

I find it helps to organize chores into categories: things I won't do now, things I won't do later, things I'll never do.

MAXINE Cartoon (Created by John Wagner)

How many times have you found yourself writing down the same steps for household routines over and over again? *Save time and mental energy by creating master lists*, such as shopping list, chore list, emergency contact list, packing list, etc. Yes, creating these lists will take some time in the short run, but they will save you time in the long run over and over. Create these lists little by little when you are preparing for or engaging in the activity, so that the steps to take are fresh in your mind. Think of it as creating a blueprint for each activity.

You will also find a sample master vacation packing list on page 125, and a sample master food shopping list on pages 66–67. Here is a sample master list for household chores.

Master Household Chores List

Write in your own tasks as well.

Daily	Weekly	Occasionally
Cook meals	Dust	Iron
Laundry	Clean bathrooms	Wash windows
Pet care	Change sheets	Clean appliances:
Clean kitchen	Vacuum floors	Fridge
Tidy up	Wash floors	Oven
Sweep floors	Water plants	Microwave
Make beds	Take out trash	Fans
	Lawn care	Wash walls & ceilings
	Shake out rugs	Wash car
	Grocery shop	Clean under furniture
		Clean carpets
		Sort & clean:
		Drawers
		Cabinets
		Closets
		Polish silver
		Touch-up paint
		Clean furniture
		Make minor repairs
		Test smoke & CO detectors

Errands:

Procrastination: Time Management's Enemy

Ah, procrastination. Most people experience it at one time or another. Procrastination can be a deep-seated problem involving fear of failure or success, or a natural result of overload. Regardless of why you are experiencing procrastination, there are ways to overcome it! How you choose to overcome procrastination depends on the task involved, the people involved, and the underlying reason for the procrastination.

Take a look at the following strategies, and see which help conquer your procrastination the next time it rears its ugly head.

Get Started

Stalled out on a task or project? Take a cue from Nike, and "Just Do It!" Once you get started, you gain momentum and energy. Usually, all of the thinking about and dreading the task is worse than actually doing it!

Don't Start at the Beginning

Sometimes, you get tripped up on how to start an activity. Well, oftentimes there is no rule that says you have to start at the beginning. Start somewhere else if that is easier, then work your way back to the beginning once you've made some progress and gained a handle on the task or activity.

Take it One Step at a Time

Many people procrastinate simply because the task seems too formidable, or there isn't enough time to do it now. But you don't have to do it all now! Break the task into small, manageable segments, each with its own end in sight. This encourages motivation and discourages procrastination.

Involve Other People

Being accountable to someone else can be a very effective way to overcome procrastination. Collaborate by working with someone else to get the task or activity started and finished faster. Two minds (or pairs of hands) can be better than one! Or you can assemble an entire team if that is feasible. You can also barter with someone to do the parts of the task or activity that you don't like or are not good at, and then in turn, do something you do like or are good at for him or her. Lastly, you can give the task or activity away altogether by delegating it to a family member, friend, employee, or co-worker.

Set a "Finish Line"

Ever notice that we call the due date for a task or activity a "deadline?" We attach a negative concept to the tasks and activities we want to accomplish. When you complete a task or activity, it is not dead, merely completed. Think instead of reaching a finish line, so that you view your task or activity as a game or race. On your mark, get set, go!

Cause and Effect

Use good old behavior modification tactics. Don't allow yourself to do something else until you start or finish your project. Or set up a reward that you treat yourself to once you reach a certain milestone in the project or at its completion.

Review the preceding tips for overcoming procrastination, and take note here of which ones you will implement and how.

Time Management Tips and Tricks: Small Steps Can Make a Big Impact!

Here are some quick time management tips and tricks that you can use to get a handle on your schedule and hopefully "find" time here and there. They may seem like small steps, but they can make a big impact, especially if you do more than one tip!

Take 15

At the end of every day, take 15 minutes to put things in order. At home before you go to bed at night, spend 15 minutes picking up stray items and putting them back into their proper homes. At the office, put away files that are no longer in use, plug in to-dos on your daily list from your master one, take out files to be used the next day, etc. That way, you come into a clean, ready-to-work environment.

Prepare for Your Morning the Night Before

Gather everything you will need, such as your pocketbook, briefcase, knapsack, keys, etc. If you have a "home" for these things near your entryway, you will never have a problem scurrying around for them when you are leaving the house. Choose your clothes and set them out in a convenient location for dressing. Get out what you need to quickly and easily prepare breakfast. And be sure to pack your lunch the night before also!

Jot it Down

Spending too much time trying to recapture your thoughts after dealing with interruptions? When interrupted, get back on track by taking a moment to jot down the very next thing you were going to do before you handle the interruption (if you decide to take it at all!). This one technique can help you not have to backtrack, which can save a lot of time per day!

Set up a Gift-Giving Zone

Buy cards in advance for many types of occasions and even consider some generic gifts for house warming, birthdays, and baby showers. Keep the items together in a gift, card, and gift-wrapping station with everything you need at your fingertips. Many people store their gift-giving station in a closet, pantry, or in the basement so that it does not take up precious real estate in the home, but is still easily accessible for those occasions when you need it.

Record TV Shows

Turn on the television only when your show is scheduled to begin and turn it off when it is over. Don't think it will make a big difference? Turning the television off one hour per week gives you 52 extra hours in a year. That's a lot of time! Some people record shows even if they are home in order to avoid commercials, not interrupt themselves, and save the show for when it is most convenient for them to watch.

Listen and Learn

Listen to audiobooks or podcasts for your commute (learn a foreign language, engage in professional or personal development, read novels, etc.), or consider carrying a digital audio recorder to dictate work assignments or even personal ideas.

Portable Reading

Carry a "to read" file with you for those times when you are waiting in line, waiting at the doctor's office, on the subway, etc. If the reading material sits in a pile at home, it hardly ever gets read!

Delivery Anyone?

Use services that offer delivery, like office supplies, dry cleaning, laundry, supermarkets, pharmacies, restaurants, etc.

Organized Errands

Do all of your errands at one time, starting farthest from your house and ending up closest to home.

Match Other's Tardiness or Enjoy "Found" Time

If there is a certain someone who is always 15 minutes late to meet you, instead of getting there on time and fuming over his or her tardiness, also arrive 15 minutes late, using that time for other tasks and activities on your to-do list. Or arrive on time and steal 15 minutes of "found" time. You may wind up thanking your chronically late friend rather than being mad at him or her!

Call & Confirm

Call ahead before going to the store to see if they have what you need, call to confirm appointments before you show up, call to see if the restaurant has seating. Save yourself unnecessary drives.

Review the preceding time management tips, and take note here of which ones you will implement and how.

Voilà! Time management in a nutshell. Remember, your role in the time management game is a crucial one. Take back control!

Notes

Each small task of every day is part of the total harmony of the Universe.

ST. THERESA OF LISIEUX

CHAPTER 3:
organizing at home

Have nothing in your house that you do not know to be useful or believe to be beautiful.

WILLIAM MORRIS

Visualize an Organized Home

What does an organized home mean to you? What does it look like? How does it function? Picture an organized home in your mind. Can you see it?

Now, describe what that organized home looks and feels like, and how it functions.

Compare what you visualized as an organized home to the following and see if any of the characteristics of an organized home match. Check off any that you "saw" in your vision.

- ☐ Eating at the table without having to move papers to another location.
- ☐ Having a spot for your kids to leave their school papers where they don't get lost in the shuffle.
- ☐ Having a memory box for each child with only the most important and precious papers and items in it, instead of an overflowing bin of school papers and artwork.
- ☐ Being prepared for school and work the evening before.
- ☐ Maintaining a paper management system for daily mail.
- ☐ Paying bills on time.
- ☐ Involving all family members in maintaining an organized environment.

☐ Tracking the family's activities on one master calendar.

☐ Keeping dirty laundry in hampers or in a sorting system in the laundry room, and having clean laundry promptly organized by person in the laundry room or put away in closets and drawers.

☐ Having closets, cabinets, and drawers that are not overflowing, so items can be found by all family members.

☐ Walking through the house without tripping over clutter.

☐ Entertaining without having to do the mad rush of temporarily moving clutter to prepare for guests.

Take a moment to write your thoughts about your results.

Welcome! The Entryway

Depending on your home, the entryway can be an entire mudroom with lots of space, a formal foyer at the front of your house, a breezeway from the garage, or a portion of a hall in a small apartment. Regardless of where it is, or its size, if it is organized your homecoming will always be less stressful, not to mention that you may actually want to have visitors over!

Tips and To-Dos for an Organized Entryway

Check boxes next to tips you intend to try, and shade in boxes when tips are implemented.

- [ ] Put everything you need to grab in the morning in the same place every night: keys, briefcase, purse, cell phone, lunch bag, etc. You can save 15 minutes by investing five the night before…and save a whole lot of stress too!

- [ ] If you have children, create a launching and landing pad for school supplies, backpacks, shoes, and sports equipment. (See page 130 for more details.)

- [ ] Put accessories (gloves, hats, scarves) in containers. Organize by family member or by accessory category, whichever makes the most sense for your home and family.

- [ ] If you have a front or back hall closet, use it for everyday outerwear for the current season only. Add a shelf, a shoe rack, and any other organizing products that help contain clutter. If there is room, you can even add a hanging shelf system (a canvas one will work fine) for accessories such as hats, umbrellas, and scarves to be handy.

- [ ] If you are not lucky enough to have a closet in your entryway, then you need to create the storage system by using cubbies, pegs, a bench, a shoe drying mat, umbrella stand, hanging mail rack with key hooks, etc. Make this the spot for outerwear, knapsacks, briefcases, keys, etc.

- [ ] You may opt for a hall table if you have room for a mail, key, wallet, and cell phone area.

- [ ] Another option: Put all keys in a small container or decorative key cabinet, and label them either with a permanent marker or key tabs, so that you know what each key corresponds to. As a security measure, you may want to use a code instead of labeling the keys "back door," "garage," etc.

- [ ] This may be a good place for a "return and repair center" if you have space. It is where you keep items that need to be returned to the store, the library, or to rightful owners from whom you borrowed them. Likewise, you can store items to be repaired here so that you are reminded to grab them as you head out the door.

The more of these tips you implement, the more welcoming and less cluttered your entryway will be.

Living and Family Rooms

Many homes have both family rooms and living rooms these days. Most families do not need both. The family room winds up being the one most used by modern day families (along with the kitchen— more on that multi-purpose room later!). Therefore, in some homes the living room is used only for entertaining. If that is the case, and you like it that way, fine. But if you hardly ever entertain and are running out of space in your home, consider re-purposing the formal living room into a space more relevant to your needs, such as a home office, playroom, or extra bedroom if possible.

Think about what your family does in the family room. Knowing how your family uses the space will help you determine what items need to be stored there, and whether other items can be relocated to other places in the house. Is the room used for playing games, relaxing, watching TV, listening to music, napping, entertaining, or reading? Customize the space depending on how it's used.

Tips and To-Dos for an Organized Family Room

Check boxes next to tips you intend to try, and shade in boxes when tips are implemented.

☐ Use the largest piece of furniture, usually the sofa, as a room divider if you need to break up the space and have it serve two functions (TV viewing area and computer area for homework, for example).

☐ Use furniture that also increases your storage capacity—coffee and end tables with storage, armoires or entertainment centers with drawers or shelves, and ottomans that open for extra storage.

☐ If you are lucky enough to have a window seat, use it for storage. If you don't have a window seat, consider adding one. They are a nice design element, and their storage possibilities are many. They can even be configured with rails to store files if necessary!

☐ Consider adding shelves to walls. Many urban dwellers use their walls to store books, CDs, and other collectibles. An added bonus is that open shelving forces you to keep the items neat and organized. You can store items in attractive containers (baskets or leather bins) if they are out on a shelf.

☐ Use a remote control caddy to store remotes and TV guides.

☐ Use a magazine rack for current catalogs and magazines only.

☐ Add a stylish bin or basket for paper recycling if you read magazines and newspapers in this room.

Kitchens

The kitchen is usually the multi-purpose room of the house—phone center, study hall, party hangout, cooking station, and dining area. Also, the kitchen is the area where many people tend to accumulate huge volumes of items they never use.

Another organizing issue in kitchens is that, very often, items are put away according to where they fit, not where they're used. It's better to store related items together, and most frequently used items in accessible places. Store frequently used items in the kitchen cabinets and shelves that are between your knees and shoulders for easy access. Items that you use less frequently can be stored below or up high, or even in another location like a nearby pantry, or a section of the garage or basement.

Tips and To-Dos for an Organized Kitchen

Check boxes next to tips you intend to try, and shade in boxes when tips are implemented.

☐ Set up a food prep and cooking zone. Use the area with the most counter space between the sink and refrigerator, or the sink and stove to prep food to be cooked. Use the counters and drawers closest to the stove to store cooking utensils, knives, oven mitts, and potholders. Or try a magnetic strip mounted to the wall behind the stove to keep cooking utensils and knives right where you need them. This is a popular European design that is used in most professional cooking spaces, including restaurants, and is highly functional and very modern looking.

☐ Add open shelves for cookbooks, serving platters, vases, and baskets. This is another popular European design where kitchen shelves are left exposed with no doors. Or use cabinets with glass front panels. Being able to see your items in plain view will force you to keep things neat and organized.

☐ Install organizational tools, such as wire shelving on the inside of cabinet and pantry doors, to increase storage space.

☐ If possible, adjust shelves in cabinets to eliminate wasted space. Don't accept the shelving configuration installed by the manufacturer or kitchen contractor if it's not efficient.

☐ Add shelf expanders that stand on cabinet shelves to double storage capacity.

☐ Use "step up" racks, which are especially good for spices and canned goods.

☐ Consider a lid organizer for pot and pan covers, and even baking sheets.

☐ Hang a wall grid or ceiling rack for pots and pans, which is a European design that is both stylish and utilitarian. This will free up a lot of space in lower cabinets that no longer are stuffed with pots and pans.

☐ Install a built-in microwave to save counter space, and under-the-cabinet versions of other appliances as well.

☐ Install a freestanding shelving unit, like a stylish baker's rack, in the kitchen or in a nearby closet or pantry to add storage space in a vertical footprint. Or use a wheeled cart with storage space below. Because it's portable, you can store it out of the way when not needed.

☐ Use sliding wire baskets under the sink for cleaning supplies and your garbage/recycling cans. If not, a cleaning caddy works well so you can carry it around the house when cleaning and put it back easily.

☐ Use a lazy Susan or plastic turntable in corner cabinets to access hard-to-reach back areas.

☐ Install a grocery bag dispenser for plastic bags that mounts inside a cabinet or pantry door.

☐ Use drawer dividers for utensils and that messy junk drawer!

Food, Menus, and Groceries

Watching what you eat? Then get organized! Spending some time organizing your food for the day can help cultivate healthy eating habits.

☐ Use the grocery list template on the following pages to create a grocery list of your most used food and kitchen items, and make 52 copies, one for each week. Place on the refrigerator and check off weekly what you need instead of writing out a new list each time. If you want to go high tech, keep the master grocery list on your computer and print it out so you can easily change it week to week. Or better yet, put it on your smart phone so you always have it with you!

☐ Make double portions when you cook, and freeze the leftovers for meals at a later date.

☐ Purge old cookbooks and recipes that you don't use. You need only one all-purpose cookbook and a few favorite recipes. These days you can get recipes online in a flash!

☐ Get a plastic accordion-style coupon organizer to store coupons, your shopping list, takeout menus, etc.

Master Food Shopping List

Customize this list, adding items to check off in their respective categories, and make copies.

Remember: ☐ Returnables ☐ Recyclable bags ☐ Reusable bags ☐ Coupons

Produce

Frozen

Deli

Meats, Poultry, & Fish

Refrigerated

Baking

Cookies & Crackers

Beverages

Breads & Pastas

Toiletries

Paper Goods

Other

What's In Your Memory Box?

Creating an Organized Home for Your Prized Possessions

There are two things to aim at in life: first, to get what you want, and after that, to enjoy it.

LOGAN PEARSALL SMITH

A memory box is a container in which each family member can store his or her most treasured possessions. The size should be big enough to fit the prized possessions, but small enough to grab and carry out of the house in case of an emergency. The actual container can be a no-nonsense functional type, like a plastic bin, or it can be a lovely decorated stylish box, bin, or basket. My personal memory box is an old trunk that has handles on the side to carry it in the event of an emergency evacuation.

The location for storing the memory box is also a personal decision. Often, because of the confidential or personal nature of the items in the box, it makes the most sense to store each person's memory box in his or her bedroom, at the top or bottom of a closet, under the bed, etc. But some choose to store all of the memory boxes for the family in a basement or attic, so that they do not take up precious space in the living areas of the home, and can be grabbed easily in one fell swoop if need be.

What goes in a memory box? Well, that is up to you, of course. But here are some ideas.

- Start a memory box for your children's prized artwork, sentimental childhood possessions, and schoolwork. You can have a master memory box, and one for the current school year. At the end of the school year, you and your child can revisit the year, purging any items that are not vital enough to go in the master memory box.

- If you have a few sentimental articles of clothing that you just can't part with, but don't wear, store them in your memory box.

- Want to revisit your love life? Store old love letters, poems, your corsage or boutonniere from your high school prom, a playbill from the first date with your spouse, etc.

- If you plan to store documents or photographs, consider putting them in an archival quality document or photo box inside the larger memory box. This will ensure papers and photos do not get destroyed over time.

- If an item is much too large to fit into the memory box, and you can bear to part with it, take a photo of the item and store the photo with a description of the item in the box. This works well for items that you are keeping merely out of obligation. For example, that hideous painting your aunt made for you that you will never hang up! Take a photo, write a note saying, "Aunt Gertrude meant well" and donate the painting to someone who will appreciate its unrecognized beauty.

- Certain items probably should NOT be kept in the memory box.
  - I would not recommend storing vital documents, such as your will or birth certificate, in the memory box. Those items should be stored either in a safety deposit box at the bank, or at home in a fire resistant box.
  - Stuck in a relationship rut? It might be time to throw out those old love letters. Experts say keeping mementos that have bad memories attached to them can psychologically weigh you down. Get rid of the negative clutter!

People are often surprised to hear that I, being a professional organizer, have a memory box. Yes, I do! Organizing is about decluttering your life of the stuff that does not serve your goals, and letting the cream rise to the top. It is about giving your favorite possessions a place of value in your home and life. My personal memory box includes select sentimental items, including my handwritten journals; my baton (yes, I was a baton twirler—don't laugh!); my middle school graduation dress (loved it!); love letters from my husband; cards and letters from loved ones who have passed away, including my beloved mother; and poems that I wrote while growing up.

A memory box gives a place of honor to precious items that may be scattered around the house, and stores them conveniently together, safe from loss or wear and tear.

So, what's in *your* memory box?

Fill Your Memory Box

If you already have a memory box, list the contents of it here. If you don't have one yet, get going! Create a memory box, and list the contents here as you put them in their new special home.

Sentimental childhood possessions

Mementos and souvenirs

Letters and cards

Kids' artwork

Documents and photographs

Kids' schoolwork

Bedrooms

Bedrooms often become disorganized due to clothes. If you have a closet and chest of drawers to store your clothes, use them! Clothes do not belong on the floor, on a chair, on an unused treadmill, or thrown on your bed.

Tips and To-Dos for Organized Bedrooms

Check boxes next to tips you intend to try, and shade in boxes when tips are implemented.

- [ ] Use under-the-bed space for storage of items you do not need out but want access to more frequently than storing them in the basement or attic. Off-season clothes and linens are a good choice. There are clear storage containers made for under the bed that are open on both sides and are on wheels. If your bed is not high enough, use bed risers.

- [ ] Use drawer dividers in dressers to contain small undergarments. They come in all shapes, sizes, and materials.

- [ ] Try to designate no more than three categories per dresser drawer and when you must combine more than one category, make sure they are related or make sense. Save the bottom, hard to access drawers for items used the least.

Unfortunately, bedrooms often serve as a makeshift home office if there is no actual designated home office room. Think carefully about whether this is a good idea. Home offices usually include a computer, a paper management system, and filing cabinets. Do you really want those items in your bedroom where you should be relaxing and sleeping?

Tips and To-Dos for Overhauling Your Clothes Closet

Check boxes next to tips you intend to try, and shade in boxes when tips are implemented.

- [ ] Remove everything from your closet.

- [ ] Create four piles: Keep, Donate, Toss, Tailor/Clean. If you haven't worn it in a few seasons, get rid of it! Remember to keep track of what you donate and get a receipt for a tax deduction.

- [ ] Try on everything in your keep pile and decide item by item if it is really a keeper. If you are unsure, try it on and look in a mirror. Or better yet, ask a kind but honest friend to come over and give you his/her opinion as you conduct a mini fashion show. Or splurge on the ultimate—hire an image or wardrobe consultant to help you.

- [ ] If you have a few sentimental favorites you can't part with but won't wear, store them in your memory box or out-of-season storage area.

- [ ] Once you've pared down, give your closet an orderly flow. Organize by garment type (shirts, pants, dresses, suits), season (current in most accessible location), color (only if that appeals to you), use (work versus casual), size (good for babies and little kids who grow out of sizes easily)—whatever makes the most sense for your lifestyle.

- [ ] Consider storing your off-season clothing in a separate location if they take up too much room. Dress clothes/evening wear used occasionally can also go elsewhere.

- [ ] Use wooden hangers for suits and slacks, clear plastic swivel hangers for shirts, and padded hangers for lingerie and delicate items.

- [ ] Be ruthless about weeding out your clothes on a regular basis, at least whenever there is a change of seasons. Keep an empty bin, bag or basket at the bottom of your closet for items to be donated. It will encourage you to get rid of those clothes that you don't love, don't wear often, are out of style, or that don't fit—or that are just plain ugly!

- [ ] Come across a prom dress or bridesmaid dress while sorting through your closet? Outfit a local drama department or community theater! They're always looking for great costumes. And, really, are you going to wear them again?

- [ ] Assign a specific function to each closet: everyday clothes, off-season, evening wear, etc.

- [ ] The average clothes closet is not designed to maximize space. The single rod and shelf configuration is impractical for most wardrobes and wastes a huge amount of space. Configure your closets with double hanging on one side, and shelves on the other, if possible.

- [ ] Use the space below the hanging clothes for shoes, accessories, etc. or even to slip a small chest of drawers underneath.

- [ ] If you have several hanging rods, one behind the other, use the back rod for off-season clothes.

- [ ] Use doors and walls for storage: attach hooks, and add shelves.

- [ ] Use clamp-on shelf dividers, which separate stacks of garments and keep them straight on shelves without sides.

Kids' Rooms and Playrooms

From when kids are a young age, their rooms are almost like college dorm rooms: multi-purpose spaces where they sleep, study, hang out, and do homework. With all of these activities going on in one (usually small) space, the rooms must be organized in order to avoid clutter pileup. Remember what a kindergarten classroom looked like? Use those same principles at home! Make cleanup easy by having a place for everything, and make organizing fun by using cool bins, containers, and labels.

Tips and To-Dos for Organized Kids' Rooms and Playrooms

Check boxes next to tips you intend to try, and shade in boxes when tips are implemented.

☐ Limit the amount of toys so that your children can focus and enjoy the toys they have. Child psychologists state that most children have too many toys, which can cause over-stimulation. Rotate them in and out of use.

☐ Purge toys that have been outgrown, broken, or never used. Donate, and include your child in the process so that he or she learns the process of clearing clutter and helping needy families. Bringing children with you when you donate items helps them learn to part with things and helps them to see how others benefit.

☐ Consider making the bedroom a toy-free zone, except for a current toy or game in use. Store toys and games in the playroom, basement, or hall closet instead.

☐ Every child's room should include a bookcase. It keeps books contained in one place and encourages reading as a habit. You can store current books on a bottom shelf and less frequently used books, toys/games, and stuffed animals/knickknacks on upper shelves.

☐ Limit the amount of stuffed animals you permit to pile up in your kids' bedrooms. Stuffed animals and other knickknacks can go in a mesh net or "hammock" hung from the ceiling in the corner. You can also install a shelf just below the ceiling around the perimeter of the room. Another simple solution is to use a clear over-the-door shoe bag for small toys or stuffed animals.

☐ Sort clothing regularly. Clothes that don't fit can be saved for younger children or donated.

☐ Use the "One In, One Out" rule to curb clutter growth: For every new item that comes in, one item must go out!

☐ If your child does not have a lot of hanging clothes, use one side of the closet for shelves or rolling drawers to store toys, games, school supplies, arts and crafts, etc. The advantage to drawer units on wheels is that you can store them in the closet and take them out only when needed.

- [ ] Use clear bins with labels. This will help children to be able to see what's inside each bin, and will reinforce learning how to read.

- [ ] If your child cannot seem to find the hamper, consider using one that is fun. For example, install a basketball hoop over the laundry basket for a young boy and watch the dirty clothes actually make it into the hamper!

- [ ] Consider scanning some schoolwork and even artwork into the computer and purging the original. You can also take photos of bulky items—such as art projects—and save the photo rather than the dust collector. Use artwork for gift-wrap or cards!

Notes:

Bathrooms and Linen Closets

Bathrooms usually do not have a ton of room, which causes clutter to build up on counters and on floors. If you are lucky enough to have a vanity with drawers, shelves, or cabinets, use it to store bathroom essentials. If not, you need to be creative.

Tips and To-Dos for Organized Bathrooms and Linen Closets

Check boxes next to tips you intend to try, and shade in boxes when tips are implemented.

- [ ] Consider an over-the-toilet style étagère with shelves on which to store bathroom items.
- [ ] Mount a shelving unit to a wall if space allows to store bathroom items.
- [ ] Mount a medicine cabinet or vanity above the sink with a mirror for extra storage.
- [ ] Use a shelf expander under the bathroom sink to increase space by adding an extra shelf.
- [ ] Add a pull-out bin under the sink to easily reach items that you use on a daily basis.
- [ ] Install a hook on the inside of the cabinet door to hang a blow-dryer or curling iron.
- [ ] Install towel bars on walls and hooks behind the bathroom door for towels and bathrobes.
- [ ] Use baskets on the floor and roll towels to maximize storage.
- [ ] Use a makeup caddy with handles that can be stored under the sink or in a drawer. You can also use this for select everyday toiletries. Consider a clear, plastic kind so that you can easily see and grab what you need.
- [ ] Install a corner shelf in the shower to store shampoo and soap.
- [ ] Install a storage system that hangs from the shower rod or shower head to store shampoo and soap.
- [ ] If you have a linen closet in the bathroom, designate some shelves for bathroom toiletries and other shelves for linens and towels.
- [ ] If your linen closet is in a nearby hallway, use it mostly for linens and towels. Store only overflow bathroom items and toiletries outside the bathroom. That way, the essential items for the bathroom are in easy reach.
- [ ] Install shelf expanders in the linen closet to double storage space by adding shelves between existing ones.
- [ ] If your linen closet has wasted space below the bottom shelf, use a freestanding shelving unit, install more shelves, or buy a rolling bin or cart that rolls into the bathroom for use but is stored in the closet.

☐ If you are lucky enough to have a linen closet in your bathroom and an additional one in the hallway, you can use one for bathroom essentials and toiletries, and the other for towels and linens. Or you can repurpose the hallway closet altogether, using it for whatever you need to store in that location. Be creative! I have converted linen closets to gift giving and wrapping centers, off-season clothing storage, crafts storage, etc. The opportunities are many, so use your imagination!

Laundry

Tips and To-Dos for an Organized Laundry Area

Check boxes next to tips you intend to try, and shade in boxes when tips are implemented.

☐ Set up typical laundry-related zones in the laundry room and throughout your home so that you are ready to tackle the laundry.

- Hamper center(s)
- Sorting center
- Drying center
- Ironing center

☐ If you have space in the laundry room, set up bins for sorting, a hanging rod, wooden or plastic drying rack, or a telescoping retractable rack for clothes that can't go in the dryer, and baskets or bins with categories of clean clothes to be brought back to each location of home.

☐ Add shelves or cabinets above the machines for laundry cleaning supplies. If no room, add a freestanding cabinet or shelves on wheels next to the machines.

☐ Designate specific days of the week to do laundry so that you can stay on track. You may need to schedule laundry as an actual appointment in order to honor it as a task or activity so that it gets done.

☐ Involve family members in pre-sorting and in the laundry process.

☐ Keep a dry cleaning bag or hamper in the closet near where you undress, in the laundry room, the hall closet, or any place where clothes are sorted.

☐ Use different hampers for different categories of clothing (by person, or lights versus darks, for example) so your clothes are pre-sorted before they get to the laundry room.

Outlying Areas—Basement/Attic/Garage

People usually just throw things in their basement, attic, and garage without any sense of order. These areas often become cluttered with sentimental items you don't use but have never parted with. It's okay to keep some sentimental items, but do so in an orderly fashion so you know what is there and can access it.

Ever notice that the expensive luxury cars and SUVs are parked outside in the driveway exposed to the elements, while the junk is taking up precious space in the garage? The U.S. Department of Energy reports 25 percent of people with two-car garages don't park any cars in there, and 32 percent park only one. Ouch! Clear the clutter and park the cars in the garage!

Tips and To-Dos for an Organized Basement, Attic, and Garage

Check boxes next to tips you intend to try, and shade in boxes when tips are implemented.

☐ Think vertical by using the wall space, especially in a garage and basement. Line the walls with floor-to-ceiling utility shelves, use hooks and pegboards to hold tools and gardening equipment, use bike racks to mount bikes off of floor, and use stackable recycling bins.

☐ In an attic, label boxes or bins and then create an index that you keep on the main living level of your home so that you don't have to climb up to see if an item is stored there.

☐ You can also create an index of stored items by zone, bin, or box for your basement, and keep it at the top of the basement stairs to avoid unnecessary trips. You can even keep these indexes or charts on your computer so that they are searchable.

☐ Organizing these outlying areas usually works best when you set up zones. Set up areas with related items in each space:

- Sporting equipment
- Workshop/Hardware
- Patio/Pool/Grill
- Gift wrap
- Pantry
- Holiday
- Laundry

- Automotive equipment
- Gardening/Lawn/Snow
- Memorabilia
- Exercise equipment
- Spare household furniture and supplies
- Trash/Recycling
- Off-season clothing

Considering holding a garage or tag sale? Think carefully! You have to lug everything outside or into the garage, tag it, put up signs and place ads, go to the bank for change on hand, and service the clients. If you want to go through all of that work, fine. But please commit to yourself that anything that does not sell, you will donate!

Photos

Many people have wonderful, precious photos that are sitting in boxes waiting to be put into photo albums. Others have hundreds of digital photos on their computer hard drive with no rhyme or reason as to how they are organized. What to do?

Tips and To-Dos for Organized Photos

Check boxes next to tips you intend to try, and shade in boxes when tips are implemented.

Printed Photos

☐ If you have loads of printed photos that have not yet been organized, start by first gathering all of the photos in one location. Next, get a bunch of inexpensive bins or boxes (shoeboxes work fine) and label them so that you can sort your photos into categories.

☐ You decide on the categories, but here are some ideas:

- Vacations
- Holidays
- By family member
- Chronologically by year
- By special event

☐ While sorting, get rid of any photos that don't make the cut.

☐ Set aside prized photos to frame.

☐ Once the sorting is complete, put the categories of photos into albums or photo boxes. Make sure the albums and photo boxes are archival quality so that the photos do not get ruined over time.

☐ Decide how you will handle new photos taken. You can start a new album or box for this year, and put all photos in it chronologically, or you can save them in a sorting bin or box for future sub-categorization that matches your existing categories.

Digital Photos

☐ If you are dealing with digital photos, start sorting into categories of folders on your computer. The categories can be similar to the ones you used for printed photos, left.

☐ Delete any digital photos that don't make the cut.

☐ Back up your digital photos using an external hard drive, CDs, or an online photo storage site.

☐ Print select photos that you want to frame or put in albums.

☐ If you want to have massive amounts of photos printed, consider using a discount digital photo printing service, or putting together online albums that come ready-made.

Notes:

Do you remember that organized home you visualized at the beginning of this chapter? Are you getting closer to creating it? Take it one step at a time day-by-day, and you will be that much closer to reaching your goal. It takes work, yes, but you can do it. Just stay the course, and don't lose sight of that organized home in your vision to keep you motivated.

Notes

As you begin changing your thinking, start immediately to change your behavior. Begin to act the part of the person you would like to become.

JOHN MAXWELL

CHAPTER 4:
organizing at work

Our life is frittered away by detail. Simplify, simplify.

HENRY DAVID THOREAU

Wouldn't it be nice to actually work less, but still be productive and meet your responsibilities? How do you think being organized at work will affect your work performance and reputation? Would you like to impress your boss, improve your relationship with clients, influence colleagues, inspire co-workers and staff, finally see the surface of your desk, and empty out your inbox? Taking an organized approach to work can enhance your career by saving time and energy, improving concentration, boosting creativity, and increasing productivity.

Interestingly, many people who are disorganized at home admit to actually being organized at work. Why might this be the case? Well, for starters, if you work outside the home in an actual office, chances are that much of the office environment—for better or for worse—is organized for you. In addition, most workers have a boss to whom they are accountable and who may also be looking over their shoulder. Some people say they are more organized at work because they spend a lot more time there than at home—a sad but often true fact of life in this day and age. Others admit that it is because they are being paid to work and feel that being organized is part of their job.

So, assuming all of this is true, why are some people still disorganized at work, and others are even more disorganized at work than at home? Work brings its own challenges. Let's take a look at the statistics, shall we?

- *The Boston Globe* reported in 2006 that 15 percent of all paper handled in businesses is lost, and 30 percent of all employees' time is spent trying to find lost documents.

- In a 2008 survey conducted by NAPO of 400 consumers, 27 percent said they feel disorganized at work, and of those, 91 percent said they would be more effective and efficient if their workspace was better organized.

- Price Waterhouse Coopers estimates that workers spend nearly 50 percent of their time looking for information, including paper documents. The average document is copied 19 times—a waste of paper, ink, and supplies.

- In 2006, Esselte Corporation conducted a survey of 2,544 office workers in the United States and Europe. The survey reported that 43 percent of the Americans surveyed described themselves as disorganized, and 21 percent have missed crucial work deadlines. Nearly half say disorganization causes them to work late at least two to three times a week. Three out of four workers surveyed worldwide agreed with this statement: "I find myself becoming more stressed when everything is a mess and I can't find important documents when needed."

The bottom line is that we are busy little beavers at work! It is not all in our heads. Therefore, we need simple and efficient strategies to manage the workload, increase our productivity, and get better organized at work.

Office Organizing Systems

One of the first mistakes that many workers make is accepting the office set-up provided by the employer or left by the previous worker of that space or office. Think about it. If you work in an office environment, when you were first shown your office, didn't you just say, "Okay, looks great" and sit down to start working? Most people do not conduct a detailed assessment of the layout, lighting, filing cabinets, paper management systems, and other organizational configurations. What the average person does is just accept the work environment as is.

With the creation of worker disability laws, some employees (and, therefore, employers) started paying attention to what they needed in order to get their work done more effectively. You need to treat your organizing systems at work the same way. What organizing systems do you need in order to improve your productivity? You work better when the layout and lighting are right, you can limit interruptions, and you have easy access to everything you need on a frequent basis.

There is no "right" way to organize a workspace. The first step is deciding what works best for you with regard to furniture and equipment. Give this some thought. Visualize the best layout.

Visualize the Ideal Office Space

What does an organized office or workspace look like to you? How does it function? Picture an organized office or workspace in your mind. Can you see it?

Now, describe what that organized office or workspace looks and feels like, and how it functions. Or better yet, draw it if possible.

As you read the following tips for an organized office or workspace, pay attention to whether any showed up when you visualized the ideal office space in the exercise above.

Office Furniture Layout

The right desk provides enough surface area to get all of your work done in a layout that allows for easy navigation of projects, paper, supplies, and electronic devices such as computer and telephone.

Check boxes next to tips you intend to try, and shade in boxes when tips are implemented.

☐ Position your desk and accompanying office furniture where you feel most comfortable; do not just blindly accept the company's or your predecessor's set-up.

☐ Invest in an ergonomically designed, comfortable chair with wheels so that you can easily roll from one end of your workspace to the other.

☐ Choose the most efficient office configuration for your needs:

- **Standard configuration**—The most basic configuration, the rectangular-shaped desk facing the door is not always the best. Think twice before facing your desk directly out the door if you are easily distracted. This is a popular office set-up in corporations, but one that does not always lend itself to peak productivity. Consider placing your desk perpendicular to the door out of the view of passersby.

- **L-shaped configuration**—An L-shaped configuration is better than a standard one, as it allows for more workspace on your desk. Float your desk in the middle of the room or perpendicular to a wall, leaving space for a filing cabinet or computer station behind or at a right angle to the desk. Or better yet, set up your desk in the corner of a room, with filing cabinets to the left and right covered by a desktop, which provides for long stretches of horizontal surface space to work on.

  - A computer workstation can free up your desktop to make room for the phone and for spreading out paperwork during work projects. Place your computer monitor on a riser on the computer workstation to free up even more workspace, or store your keyboard underneath if you don't have a slide out keyboard tray.

- **U-shaped configuration**—A U-shaped configuration maximizes workspace and storage capacity in the smallest amount of space. It includes your desk, computer workstation, and filing cabinet, with your chair in the middle of the U-shaped configuration.

Where to Place File Cabinets

Do not place file cabinets too far from your desk/work area. Keep files within arm's reach so you can work out of your files all day, retrieving and putting them back with little effort. If you have to get up to file a piece of paper, it will probably just end up in a pile on your desk.

If space allows, go vertical. Replace a two-drawer file cabinet with a four-drawer vertical model.

Lateral file cabinets are good if you need more horizontal surface space for printer, fax, or copier, but change the rails so you can file from front to back instead of side to side. (It's easier to retrieve and increases capacity.)

If you share files with an assistant, place your file cabinet near the doorway so the files are located halfway between the two of you.

Tools for an Organized Office Environment

Check boxes next to tips you intend to try, and shade in boxes when tips are implemented.

☐ Use a four-tier inbox system on or near your desk:

- **Inbox**—Unprocessed papers
- **Action**—Items that need action in order to process them
- **To File**—Papers that need to be filed in your system
- **To Read**—Magazines, industry journals, articles, etc.

☐ Use a headset for the telephone, which can free up your hands to write, and also reduces neck strain.

☐ Use a file sorter, which is great for keeping current or active projects in clear view, but neatly categorized in folders.

☐ Group reference materials, such as catalogs, trade magazines, or newsletters, in a magazine holder. These come in a variety of colors and styles to match your office environment. If you don't read this material often enough, get off the mailing lists or start recycling. Don't buy more magazine holders!

☐ Utilize binders. Store these on shelves with the binder facing out, not in a pile. Label the spines so that you can see what's inside without pulling them off the shelf. Use dividers and clear sheet protectors to categorize and protect contents.

☐ For portable organization, use clipboards or accordian-style file holders. These are good for holding your current project, or taking on the road or to meetings.

☐ Install hooks on the back of your door for coats, hats, sweaters, umbrellas, and bags.

☐ Organize supplies. Daily supplies go on your desktop or in desk drawers. Try to fit supplies in one drawer if possible, or assign drawers by category. Use drawer dividers to separate supplies and keep them neat. Store bulk supplies and less frequently used supplies in a supply cabinet/closet. Keep it organized so you can easily retrieve, put away when finished using, and order when supplies are low. Post a list or index of supplies with ordering information.

Go Vertical

No room to work on your desktop? Go vertical by using your wall or vertical container systems that take up a smaller footprint on your desk. Think wall pockets, literature sorters, tiered inbox paper holders, wall shelves, etc.

Mounted Wall Pockets

You can mount these near your desk for active files or resources that you need to keep handy. Or you can mount them near the doorway for In and Out mail. (Do not allow mail to be delivered to your actual desk, which may distract you from work and get mixed up with other papers on your desk.)

Literature Sorter

This looks like an old-fashioned mailroom slot system in which papers lay flat. It's good for storing and collating sheets and brochures, and useful for salespeople or businesses that make packets of information on a regular basis. Some people use a literature sorter to create an actual filing system if they are extremely visual, the system is a small manageable size, and the files are visible.

Overhead Bins for Small-Space Dwellers

In a cubicle, overhead bins can store books, paper, supplies, etc.

Paper Management and Filing Systems

If you were unfortunate enough to have to sit for the SAT in high school, you may remember the common advice: do not change your first answer, as it is usually the right one. You can say the same thing when it comes to filing systems. I often will say to a client when they are having a hard time choosing a name for a file, "Quick, what file name would you think to look for this paper under?" I am trying to make my clients use free association, and not over-think the naming process.

File names are important only when it comes to retrieval, not storage. Most people get caught up in what to name a file because they are focusing on the front end—the storage process. But filing is most important on the back end, during the retrieval process, when you need to access something quickly after time has gone by and your memory is not as fresh. The purpose of a filing system is not to put papers away—it's to be able to find them again! Even though 80 percent of what you file you will never look at again, for the remaining 20 percent you need to think retrieval, not storage, when setting up your filing system.

What to Keep and File

Carefully consider whether it's worthwhile to retain papers. Think about the cost of cabinets and the price per square foot of space taken up. Remember, 80 percent of what is filed is never retrieved again. Be ruthless with what you choose to file!

Check boxes next to tips you intend to try, and shade in boxes when tips are implemented.

☐ Identify files that can be stored in an off-site location, shredded or recycled, given to a different department or division, or scanned and stored electronically. Unused files can be boxed up and archived with a deadline to pull out and review; if still not vital, purge!

☐ Become friends with a scanner. It's a wonderful tool that can save a lot of space in the office, enabling you to store things easily in electronic format.

☐ Create a portable To Read file to carry with you when you are waiting at the doctor's office, for a meeting to begin, or when commuting by public transportation. If you pile your reading material at work, it often gets ignored until you eventually purge it.

☐ Familiarize yourself with your employer's record retention policy so you can make informed decisions as to what to keep. If there isn't a record retention policy or if you are self-employed, create your own. Use a paper value system to decide what to keep, or create your own record retention policy. In Chapter 5 (pages 111–113), you will find a detailed record retention policy for a home office. Use that as a guide to create a similar policy for record retention at work. The paper value system exercise, right, will also help.

Paper Value System List

When faced with paper that you are trying to determine if you need to retain and file, use the following list to help you.

- Do I need to keep this paper/document/file for tax or legal purposes?

- Is there a law, policy, rule, regulation, or guideline which determines how long to keep this paper/file?

- Can I shift storage responsibility of this paper/file to a different division or department within my company? If so, which?

- Can I shift storage responsibility of this paper/file to the client?

- Do I need the entire item or just a portion of it? (For example, could you cut out an article instead of keeping the entire periodical?)

- Will I really read this article/document?

- Will I ever really access this paper/file again?

- What are the consequences if I purge this paper/file?

- If I need this paper/file after I purge it, can I easily find it somewhere else within or outside of my company?

- Will I get another one of these papers at a later date (for example, association solicitations, summaries of continuing education credits, etc.)?

- Is this paper/information too old to be useful or accurate?

- Is this paper a duplicate and if so, how many do I need to keep?

- Is this paper an earlier version of a final document, and if so, do I need a paper trail of earlier versions or can I just retain the final version?

Filing Tips

- Use Straight-Line Filing within Categories. Organize the internal manila file folders in hanging folders so the tabs all have the same position (left, middle, or right) within a category. Alternate the tab position to indicate a category shift. Straight-line filing is easier on the eye, does not break the pattern if you add or remove a file after the system is created, and makes it easier to figure out which category a file belongs to based on its position.

- Assign Files a Home. If you have the space, assign a category of files to each drawer. If not, combine a few small categories to a drawer that make sense together.

- The file drawers that are part of your desk should be used for confidential, daily, or personal matters.

- If there are no drawers for filing, use file boxes/crates, accordion-style holders, wall mounted pockets, or a rolling file bin that you can slide under your desk or in a nearby corner or closet.

Maintaining the Filing System

Check boxes next to tips you intend to try, and shade in boxes when tips are implemented.

☐ Match the names of hard copy files to the ones you create on the computer so that you do not have two sets of files with different names for the same material. Do the same for file categories (e.g., clients as a folder in the computer and then files within it by client name; do the same in your hard copy files).

☐ Check to see if your employer has a standardized naming system for computer files. If not, implement your own personal computer document naming system, or consider implementing one with your department, division, assistant, etc.

☐ If there is a central file area/room, use a "checkout card" like a library system. That way, if a file is missing, it is easy to find.

☐ Consider creating a file index of your filing system in electronic format. It makes searching for a file a snap by allowing you to be able to recall the system without having to physically sift through files. It can also be accessed by multiple users and helps to avoid duplicate files, a common problem in many offices.

☐ Clean out files at the end of every project and when archiving files.

☐ Put files away at the end of each work day. (This is part of the overall 15 minutes per day of maintaining organizing systems at work, covered in detail in Chapter 7, Staying Organized.)

☐ Create new files for papers that come across your desk and do not have a home yet, but are important enough to retain.

☐ When putting papers in your To File bin/tier, use the upper right hand corner trick. Write the name of the file in the upper right hand corner of the document, or use a sticky note if you do not want to write on the actual paper. This way, when you are filing at a later date, you do not need to reprocess the paper to figure out which file it goes into. It makes your filing go a lot faster!

☐ Learn to delegate more effectively. Many people have assistants at work but don't fully utilize them. When you have a synchronized filing system, your assistant and staff cannot only find things without having to ask you, they can also help you manage your paper more efficiently.

Review the preceding tips and checklists for paper management, and take note here of which ones you will implement and how.

How to Survive the Daily E-mail Attack!

For most people these days, keeping up with the daily onslaught of e-mail is a major challenge. In fact, experts estimate that the average person receives 67.5 e-mails in a typical workday. If you multiply 67.5 by five days for 52 weeks, the average person is receiving 17,550 e-mails per year at work alone. Wow! That is a lot of e-mail. Experts further estimate that e-mail consumes an average of 13 hours per week per information worker and is often intimately intertwined with document workflow, sales, scheduling, and other business processes. Assuming that the average information worker makes $75,000 a year, the time spent on reading and answering e-mail costs a company $20,990 per worker per year. And that means that the time lost to e-mail has caused workers to shave time elsewhere, causing a productivity crunch.

So how do you survive the daily e-mail attack? The following tips will help you manage the flow of e-mail.

Check boxes next to tips you intend to try, and shade in boxes when tips are implemented.

☐ Turn off e-mail alarms and prompts through your e-mail preferences tool. Many people have alarms and prompts set to go off every few minutes upon the arrival of e-mail in their inbox. These continual interruptions make people respond like Pavlov's dogs every time they hear the "you've got mail" chime. Turning off the chime will keep you from interrupting what you were doing to read e-mail.

☐ Plan for e-mail reading and responding in your daily schedule. Create a proactive method of managing e-mail by setting up time in your day dedicated to it. Do not check e-mail the first thing in the morning, or you risk becoming reactive. Instead, spend the first hour working on the most important project or planning your day out.

☐ Estimate the amount of time you are spending on e-mail now, and cut that time in half. Deadlines usually make most people more efficient. You may want to spend half of your allocated e-mail time in the morning, and the other half after lunch or before you finish working for the day. The time constraint forces you to prioritize. The e-mails that do not get answered are probably not that important and, thus, deleted or archived in file folders for future use.

☐ Create e-mail folders, and direct the flow of e-mail. Create folders in your e-mail system that mirror your paper filing system to reinforce storage and retrieval of important information. In addition, create the folders to reflect your active projects and change your e-mail settings to direct e-mail that contains project-related language to those folders within your inbox. Added bonus: Many e-mail systems impose limits on inbox size, but not in a folder.

- [ ] Use computer storage folders. For e-mails that need to be kept for a longer period of time, create an electronic filing cabinet, with electronic folders for category names that match the physical files. Use a word processing system that your company utilizes and backs up often.

- [ ] Save the most recent only. Delete the earlier string of e-mails and just keep the most current one to avoid saving redundant e-mails.

- [ ] Save just the attachment. If the e-mail has an attachment and that is all you need, save only the attachment and delete the e-mail.

- [ ] Control the flow of the e-mail exchange. People often feel they must respond to e-mail instantly. Take time to consider your response and slow the flow of e-mail when an immediate response is unnecessary.

- [ ] Refrain from sending irrelevant e-mail. Be careful not to send e-mail just because it's quick and convenient. The same rules apply to e-mail as regular correspondence—if it doesn't have to be said, don't say it.

- [ ] Create templates. If you frequently send the same types of e-mails, create templates that you can use over and over (changing only the specifics each time).

- [ ] Create an e-mail ritual. Every Friday before you leave the office, be ruthless about deleting e-mails no longer needed, saving those you need for a week or longer to e-mail folders, saving those you need even longer to your computer, and reviewing those in the e-mail folders to delete any no longer necessary. Make this a weekly habit and your e-mail will be a lot more manageable. You can also do the same thing at the end of every day if you so choose.

Many people are familiar with the above tips, but few actually implement them, leaving them to be reactive instead of proactive. Organizing your e-mail, like any other organizing behavior, allows you to be more productive and better utilize your time and energy. So stop the madness and do what it takes to control your e-mail. Remember, e-mail is supposed to be an electronic communications tool to assist you, not drive you crazy!

Avoid Getting Sidetracked—Own Your Interruptions

Imagine you are on a roll, engrossed in a project, in the "flow." All of a sudden, the phone rings, an e-mail alarm goes off, a colleague is standing in your doorway, a fax is coming over the machine, etc. Ugh, interruptions! If you didn't define all of those as interruptions, think again.

Experts estimate that the average amount of time that people spend on any single activity at work before being interrupted or before switching activities is about three minutes and five seconds. Some people find this number to be extremely high, others find it low. It depends on what your definition of an interruption is. My definition is anything that you didn't want or expect to happen at that time. I equate an interruption to a weed in my garden; if it doesn't belong there, or if I don't want it there, it is a weed and must be dealt with. Same with an interruption.

So how do you avoid getting sidetracked? Own your interruptions if you can. It is not always easy, and it depends on what your job is and who is interrupting you, but try it!

Own Your Interruptions

Start to think of an interruption as an offer, and your decision as to whether you will take the interruption as a counter-offer. It is okay to say, "Thanks for your call/visit. I do want to speak with you, but now is not a good time. Can we talk/meet at 2:00 PM instead?" There. You just counter-offered.

Grade Your Interruptions

Let's face it—some interruptions are more important than others. You probably need to take interruptions from certain people like your boss or a sick child, but be selective. If an interruption comes in that does not make the grade, don't take it!

Create Do-Not-Disturb Time

Screen calls, or set up times of the day when you answer and return calls and let that be known to friends, family, and work colleagues. When working on a tight deadline, utilize a "do not disturb" sign, close your office door, set "office hours" for visitors and colleagues, or go work in a conference room, library, or coffee shop where you can hide. When I was practicing law, I often escaped to another location when writing an important court brief, or closed my door and left a sign-up sheet for people who stopped by, explaining that I was on deadline and when I would surface for air.

Use a Post-it Note Wisely

Before you take an interruption, write down the very next action you were planning to take. Often, the interruption itself is not as bad as playing catch-up after it. Taking the time to write down what you need to get back to can help you save precious time.

Plan for Interruptions

If you work in an interruption-rich culture, you can only plan out 50 percent of your time to allow for 50 percent interruptions. For example, if your job is to put out "fires" all day, you can't avoid interruptions, as they are exactly what you should be handling. An example of this would be a sales manager in a car dealership whose job is to support the sales team on the floor, and to control and manage issues as they arise. This individual will be less able to avoid interruptions and should plan for them in his or her schedule, by blocking out time before or after "floor" time to get his or her project-related work done.

Stop the Interrupter

It is worth noting that supposedly 80 percent of our interruptions come from 20 percent of the people we come into contact with. Try to identify the frequent interrupters and start coming up with ways to head them off. If you know someone always calls you to confirm a meeting, send a quick text/e-mail to let him or her know you are still on as scheduled. Or better yet, explain that it is your policy not to miss meetings, that you do not need a reminder (you have your smart phone for that!), and that you will call in the rare event you need to cancel. Start taking control of the interruptions before they occur.

Now, go forth and "own" those interruptions so you can get some work done!

Notes:

Getting organized at work may be a challenge, but it is not impossible. Follow the above tips, invest in some smart organizing tools, and give some thought to your workspace layout and filing and e-mail systems.

Before you know it, you will be able to leave work on time…or even early! Now, wouldn't that be nice?

Notes

Be regular and orderly in your life so that you may be violent and original in your work.

GUSTAVE FLAUBERT

CHAPTER 5:

organizing your paper, bills, & finances—oh my!

What the world really needs is more love and less paperwork.

PEARL BAILEY

Visualize the Ideal Paper Management and Bill Paying System

Wouldn't it be nice to have a paper management and bill paying system that works? To be able to not only find your bills, but pay them on time? To have a better idea of what papers to keep and for how long? What does an organized paper management and bill paying system look like to you? How does it function? How could it change your life and your finances?

Picture an organized paper management and bill paying system in your mind. Can you see it? Now, describe what that organized paper management and bill paying system looks and feels like, and how it functions.

Compare what you visualized to the following and see if any of the characteristics of an organized paper management and bill paying system match. Check off any that you "saw" in your vision.

- [ ] Maintaining a paper management system for daily mail.
- [ ] Having a system for every piece of paper that comes into your home.
- [ ] Having a system for discarding paper that is obsolete, duplicated, or no longer needed.
- [ ] Establishing record retention guidelines as to what papers should be kept and for how long.
- [ ] Paying bills on time.
- [ ] Being able to gather all necessary papers in order to complete your income taxes on time.

Take a moment to write your thoughts about your results.

Why Is Record Retention and Paper Management So Important, Even in a Home Setting?

When you have a high-functioning paper management and record retention system, you will be motivated to actually process your papers and keep them organized. If you have good systems in place, you will be able to find what you need more easily and be able to do the mundane tasks, such as bill paying, with less stress. In addition, you will be better prepared at tax time, and possibly save money due to your excellent record-keeping abilities. Think about what paying your bills on time could do for your financial health. You will not be subject to late fees, which will improve your credit rating. Your improved credit score could help you get a better rate if you need a mortgage or loan. Your credit card interest rates will go down. Thus, being more organized with your paper and finances could actually save you money in the long run. And who wouldn't like to save a little more money?

If you work out of your home and take a home office deduction on your income taxes, it is vital that you maintain great records, both from a productivity standpoint and from a taxation one. Even if you are not running a "business" out of your home, you still are running the business of life, which involves constant paper flow.

Drowning in Paper Clutter? Grab a RAFT and Sail to an Organized Shore!

Paper. It should be a benign part of our lives. It means no harm, really. But somehow, when it piles up and has a paper party with its friends, it becomes dreaded clutter! What to do?

Grab a RAFT and sail to an organized shore! (Okay, technically, it should be RAFTS, plural, but that just didn't work well in the sentence.)

Sort Your Mail Daily—Use the RAFTS Method:

- **R**ecycle—Junk mail that is not confidential
- **A**ct—Bills to pay, invitations to respond to, forms to fill out, etc.
- **F**ile—Vital documents that must be kept long term (only 20 percent of paper needs to be filed; the other 80 percent is usually irrelevant and never looked at again!)
- **T**oss—If you unfortunately do not have paper recycling in your area
- **S**hred—Anything with financial or confidential information on it

Paper Management Tips

Check boxes next to tips you intend to try, and shade in boxes when tips are implemented.

☐ Designate a spot for your mail. If there is no "mailbox" in the house, you will "deliver" it to a different spot each time, or in a location that may not be best suited to paper flow (for example, the dining room table!).

☐ Keep the recycling bin, garbage, shredder, and calendar/planner nearby to be able to take immediate action. Whatever is brought in the house should be pre-sorted by recipient (family member), category (bills, reading material, catalogs, etc.) or any system that makes sense for your household. For a large household, consider separate mail slots per person.

☐ The popular admonition to touch paper only once is impractical! Aim for less than three times. Even a professional organizer touches paper more than once. (Bills for example, are removed from the mailbox, sorted over the recycling bin, put into the bill paying center in chronological order, then paid when due.) Strive for productivity, not perfection!

☐ Eliminate paper from your home or office by simply using your calendar more frequently. Instead of keeping the paper, put the information (location of meeting, for example) on your calendar and throw the paper away (or recycle!).

☐ If you have a home office, use it! Many people have an actual home office, but do not use it to process paper, which should be its very function. Put that office to use!

☐ If you do not have a home office, set up a Home Information Center in a location that makes sense for your home. A Home Information Center does not need to be a room, but can be a "hub" somewhere in the home. A likely spot may be in the kitchen, as many people do paperwork and pay bills in the "public" areas of their home. If you do realize you need more room, re-evaluate the space you have in the home. For example, if your child is away at college, repurpose the child's bedroom as a home office. To create a simple paper management system, use a four-tier tray stacking system, with the following categories: Inbox, Action, To Read, and To File. Visit your local office supply or stationery store for stackable paper trays. Remember to check the trays daily to avoid paper clutter accumulation.

☐ Start Shredding. Unfortunately, identity theft is a real and growing concern these days. To ensure against it, make sure to use a crosscut shredder. It creates tiny confetti-like pieces of paper that cannot be put back together. A single-cut shredder creates strips of paper, which can be put back together. Be sure to shred credit card offers/solicitations. Credit card fraud is the most common type of identity theft—50 percent of all cases.

Now, go find your **RAFT** and climb in. Happy sailing!

What About School Papers?

Conquer School Papers

Set up an area in your kitchen, office, or other convenient spot where your children can leave permission slips and other school materials. You can give each child a dedicated inbox and out-box, where they can put important papers to be reviewed and signed, and you can take them out, process them, and then put them in the outbox to go back to school if appropriate.

School Reference Materials

After Orientation Night, set up a school reference file or binder with all of the papers you have received, including current information about school, class lists, and after-school activities. Having one organized place to look up information saves time. If the school is very organized and has everything you need on its Web site, bookmark the Web pages you need on your computer for quick and easy access. Or simply print what you might need to refer to later and add it to the school reference binder.

Use Technology

As soon as school starts, program all important telephone numbers into your mobile phone, such as school, inclement weather, emergency pick-up person, etc. Or record these contact numbers into your daily planner or address book and keep them with you at all times.

Use Templates

Create templates of various forms for school, such as permission slips or tardy and absent forms, and make copies. Include blank areas to fill in the appropriate names and dates. Or use forms created for such purposes in family organizing binder systems.

Gather Your One-Month Reading Universe

Are you an intellectual hoarder? So many people keep stacks of newspapers, books, and magazines they hope to read "someday." Someday is here, and you haven't made time to read them yet. Perhaps you are overestimating how much one little person can read in a 30-day period.

Gather all of the reading material that crosses your path for a 30-day period in one location. Everything—newspapers, magazines, PTA newsletters, library circulars, etc. At the end of that 30-day period, take a look. This will give you a visual snapshot of how much reading material you receive and expect to read in only one month! Measure the linear feet. Go ahead. Shocking, eh? Ask yourself if it's possible to read all this in a month. The answer is most likely a resounding "No!"

Give yourself a break and stop some of the reading material from coming across your path in the first place by implementing the following tips.

- Use alternative means of information. Go online to read your favorite periodicals and blogs, listen to audiobooks while driving, and keep only a realistic amount of physical reading material. Don't forget that you can find reading material at your local library, and visit it whenever you want. Get rid of the physical clutter and free up that intellectual mind of yours to actually take in more information!

- Evaluate whether you want to continue to receive magazines and newspapers that you are not regularly reading. Cancel subscriptions, rotate them, or share with a friend or neighbor.

- Do you tear out articles from magazines and newspapers? You had every intention of reading those articles, yet there they are, still just a stack of paper. Give yourself permission to let them go (trust that the information is mostly in your head now!). Get in the habit of cutting out only those articles you know you will refer to again, and recycling the magazine itself. Set up those articles by subject matter (gardening, decorating, parenting, etc.) in your home filing system, or scan them in and create a subject matter library on your computer.

- Want to whittle down your reading material? Be clear on your goals and priorities. If this is the year you want to focus on your photography hobby and learn more about architecture, then get only magazines about those two topics. Cancel the gardening and home decorating magazines until those hobbies become a priority again. Being clear on what your interests are can be a great way to cut down on your reading material.

Review the preceding tips for streamlining reading material, and take notes here of which ones you will implement and how.

Organized Bill Paying

Not keeping track of papers can become expensive. Late fees for credit card payments make up about 70 percent of the multi-billion dollar credit card industry, rising to $18.1 billion in 2006. Set up an effective bill paying system to help avoid those late fees!

Check boxes next to tips you intend to try, and shade in boxes when tips are implemented.

☐ Create a bill-paying center in a location that is easily accessible, won't be overlooked, and is close to your paperwork. Add a calculator, stamps, envelopes, address labels, and your checkbook to complete the center.

☐ Want to pay bills on time? Keep it simple. Set up a chronological bill paying tickler system by using a simple letter sorter. Write the due date on the outside of the bill's envelope and place each bill in the sorter in reverse chronological order. That way, the one showing is the first one due and all of the bills behind it are due subsequently. You only need to keep track of the first due date. Put the system someplace that you walk by every day. If the first bill isn't overdue, the rest aren't either!

☐ You can use this chronological tickler system for more than just bills. You can add invitations, gift certificates, coupons, etc.—anything that has a due date and needs attention!

☐ Change bill due dates, if your cash flow allows, to one or two due dates per month (for example, the 1st and 15th) so you can pay bills less frequently and not have to keep track of so many dates.

☐ Pay bills online! According to a report by Javelin Strategy & Research, 53 percent of Americans currently use online banking services—rising to an estimated 67 percent by 2012. The report also estimates that 16.5 million trees would be saved every year if all Americans switched from paper bills to Internet banking.

Vital Documents

Why should you keep vital documents? These are kept to establish ownership, to establish basis (cost), to support tax deductions, and to establish or provide for a benefit. Here are some tips for keeping vital documents safe and organized.

Check boxes next to tips you intend to try, and shade in boxes when tips are implemented.

☐ Keep your will, trust, power of attorney, birth and marriage certificates, passports, insurance policies, paper bonds and stock certificates, property deeds, and other permanent records in a safe but accessible place. A safety deposit box at the bank is good, as is a fire resistant box in your home. Beware—there is no such thing as a fireproof box! The boxes will only last a few hours depending on the box's fire rating and where the fire actually burns. Also, realize that a fire resistant box that is not bolted to the floor and is not too heavy can be stolen. Make sure you keep copies of these vital documents as a back-up somewhere (with the attorney who drafted your will, with your executor, scanned into your computer, backed-up online, etc.).

☐ Make sure that someone else signs the signature card and/or has the key to the safety deposit box or it may get sealed in the event of your death while your estate goes through probate, which could take months. If a husband and wife both die, for example, and only their names are on the signature card, then the will must allow for a third party to open the box and remove its contents.

☐ Create a vital documents index so you know exactly what is in that file, fire resistant box, or safety deposit box. Or better yet, make a copy of each document stored in the vital documents section.

☐ You should also consider making copies of the contents of your wallet. That way, if your wallet is ever lost or stolen, you will know what was in it, and be able to re-create those items.

☐ Some people store their vital documents in a regular folder in their filing cabinet, and keep copies (or the originals) in a separate location.

☐ In the event that an emergency causes a very quick evacuation, the people and pets go out first, followed by the vital documents, and then the memory boxes.

Record Retention: How Long to Keep What

Here are some rules of thumb for knowing which categories of papers to keep and for how long.

Note: Always check with your accountant, attorney, financial planner and/or insurance agent before shredding vital documents! Your particular situation may require different handling than described in the general guidelines below.

Discard Monthly

- **ATM/Bank deposit slips**—Discard after you've recorded the amounts in your checkbook and reconciled them against your monthly bank statements.

- **Credit card receipts**—Discard after you've cross-checked them with your credit card statement (unless they support a tax deduction).

- **Sales receipts for minor purchases**—Discard after you've satisfactorily used the items and if they don't have warranties. If they have warranties, you should staple the receipt to the front of your warranty and then file with Manuals and Warranties. For consumables like food and gas, there is no reason to keep receipts beyond reconciling them with credit card or bank statements, unless you need them to support a business tax deduction.

- **Monthly bank and credit card statements**—Save only bank and credit card statements that support itemized tax deductions. Keep one statement at all times in the file for contact information. When the next statement arrives, file it and purge the last one.

- **Phone and utility bills**—Discard unless you need them to support a tax deduction for a home office or business. Keep one statement at all times in the file for contact information. When the next bill arrives, file it and purge the last one.

Discard Annually

- **Monthly or quarterly investment statements**—Unless you want to measure performance or track investments, you can discard the monthly statement as soon as you receive the quarterly and the quarterly as soon as you receive the annual, which clearly shows the amount you've paid in interest for the year. The annual investment statement often comes with a 1098 interest income statement, which you need for tax purposes. You may also want to set up a file to track "confirmations of sale" for when you buy and sell. This is only necessary if your investment company is not tracking these for you electronically.

- **Paycheck stubs**—Discard after you've reconciled them with your annual W-2 or 1099 forms, unless you need them to prove vesting in your employer's or a state's retirement system.

Retain for Seven Years

- **Tax returns**—IRS Publication 552 provides that you must keep tax returns for three years. However, it is advisable to keep tax returns for at least six years from the date of filing to be conservative, as the IRS has that long to audit you if they suspect you have underreported your income by 25 percent or more. The IRS retains Form 1040 forever on file. IRS Form 4506 allows a taxpayer to get details of past returns, but not supporting documentation. Therefore, if you are concerned with being audited for a fraudulent return, keep supporting documentation for at least seven years along with the actual tax return.

- **Supporting documentation for tax returns**—These documents are the most important to organizing, as they support the deductions. Set up a file called Current Year Taxes and put everything in it to prepare your taxes or you may miss deductions.

- **W-2 and 1099 forms, 1098 forms, and annual investment statements.** Retain these official forms with taxes for each respective year. If used to support tax deductions, keep year end statements from credit card companies, phone and utility bills with your tax documents.

- **Health insurance documents and receipts such as out-of-pocket medical costs and Explanation of Benefits (EOBs)**—Retain with taxes if you qualify for the medical deduction (medical out-of-pocket expenses exceeding 7.5 percent of your adjusted gross income). Some medical insurers offer the history of the EOBs online at their Web site, which alleviates you from having to keep them too.

- **Flexible Spending Account (FSA) documents**—Retain with taxes for each respective year.

- **Receipts, statements, and/or canceled checks for annual mortgage interest and property taxes, deductible business expenses, child care bills, or any other tax deductible expenses.** Retain with taxes for each respective year. There is no reason to keep checks or bank statements except to support a tax deduction (expenses, donations, etc.) or for the warranties of major purchases.

- **Year-end summaries from financial service companies**—Retain with taxes for each respective year.

- **Stock certificate that is deemed worthless**—Retain in order to justify loss on taxes.

Retain Indefinitely

- **Annual tax returns**—If you anticipate an audit, or if audited previously by the IRS.

- **Stock certificates in paper form**—Paper stock certificates are rare these days, and should be converted to electronic form.

- **Investment purchase records including confirmation slips that list the purchase price**—Retain for as long as you own the investment to establish basis.

- **Bonds in paper form**—Now only issued in electronic form. Older versions are still in paper and need to be sent in when mature.

- **Home improvement records**—Save until you sell your home. The cost of some home improvements can offset capital gains tax if your home has appreciated in value.

- **Manuals, warranties, and receipts for major purchases**—Retain for as long as you own the item or the item is under warranty, and if it exceeds the deductible of your homeowners' or renters' insurance policy.

- **Beneficiary designations**—Retain for as long as you hold the insurance policy, investment, or retirement plan.

- **Medical records for each family member**—This includes records of surgeries, blood work, major medical tests, medical history, list of medications, organ donor information, etc. Another option is to keep an online medical history of major illnesses, procedures, surgeries, medications, etc. on one of the online medical documentation sites that are now available.

Review the preceding rules of thumb for how long to keep what, and take notes here of which ones you will implement and how.

Categories of Home Files

In general, there are two different ways that you can organize your papers at home: alphabetically or by category. When files are created alphabetically there will be no consistency with respect to category. When files are created by category, then like subjects are filed together, which makes it easier to find and retrieve them.

Here is a sample list of categories to use for a home filing system. Many of these documents are now stored electronically on your computer or even online.

- **Auto**—Department of Motor Vehicles records, title and copy of registration, auto insurance policy, maintenance records, loan/financing, auto clubs like AAA
- **Career**—Résumé, references, supervisor's name, salary history, military history
- **Education**—Degrees, continuing education, certifications, transcripts
- **Financial**—Banking, tax records, investments, credit cards, credit report, retirement
- **Health**—Diet and exercise, fitness club memberships, weight loss programs
- **Home/Real Estate**—Lease agreement, contract of sale, closing documents, mortgage, home improvements and renovations, decorating, organizing, homeowner's insurance policy, household inventory
- **Insurance**—Life and disability
- **Legal or Vital Documents**—Marriage and birth certificates, Social Security card, divorce papers, custody agreement, adoption papers, passports, will, health care proxy/living will, power of attorney
- **Leisure**—Sporting events, community or family activities, restaurants
- **Manuals and Warranties**—Sub-categories for appliances, outdoor equipment, gardening, furniture, etc.
- **Medical**—Medical records, major illnesses and injuries, list of doctors, list of medications, organ donor information, treatment plans, health insurance, health care proxy/living will
- **Memory Box**—One for each family member
- **Pet**—Adoption or purchase certificate, veterinary records, vaccinations, kennel and dog walker information
- **Religion**—House of worship information, religious records
- **Taxes**—Actual returns with supporting documentation, filed by year in reverse chronological order, plus a file for current year tax deductions

- **Travel**—List of names of places visited, list of Web site addresses, day trips, travel agent contact information, airline frequent flyer programs, hotel clubs, passport if not kept with legal documents

Take notes here about categorizing your home files.

Your mission is to use this guide to an efficient paper management and bill paying system at home. It may not be easy, but this is an area where a little work will pay off in dividends on a daily, monthly, annual, and long-term basis. You will benefit in many ways by having a consistent, workable paper management and bill paying system at home. You will have more room to breathe, will be able to find papers when you need them, will pay bills on time, and will be able to easily gather documents to do your taxes. Now, doesn't that sound nice?

If you are still overwhelmed, read this chapter again at a later date. Paper is a major issue for most people, and takes a lot of effort to tame. Give yourself ample time to soak in all of the tips in this chapter and implement them slowly.

Notes

Excellence is an art won by training and habituation. We are what we repeatedly do. Excellence, then, is not an act, but a habit.

ARISTOTLE

CHAPTER 6:
seasonal organizing & special situations

Everything ends. But there are always new beginnings.

RALPH BELLAMY

Organizing your life should become an everyday habit and a way of life. Admittedly, however, there are times when being organized will be more challenging than others. For example, the holiday season is often chaotic for many, even though it is supposed to be joyful. Certain life transitions, such as searching for a job, becoming an empty nester, or retiring bring their own challenges and can cause temporary disorganization. Even happy occasions, such as getting married, or planning a vacation, can throw the most organized people off balance. This chapter is devoted to those seasonal organizing times and special situations that warrant particular attention.

Got Clutter? Do the Spring Fling!

Spring marks the transition from winter into summer. It is a time that most of us equate with renewal, increasing day length, and a symbolic changing of the seasons. Spring is seen as a time of growth, when new life (both plant and animal) is born. The term is also used more generally as a metaphor for the start of better times. For many, it is also a time for cleaning and organizing—i.e., the Spring Fling!

During the winter, we tend to stockpile. It is in our nature. Chances are you've got some clutter left over at work, at home, in your car, on your computer, and in your head. This is an ideal time to do some eliminating. The old adage, "Out with the old, in with the new" definitely applies this season.

Tips and To-Dos for Clearing the Clutter

Check boxes next to tips you intend to try, and shade in boxes when tips are implemented.

☐ Purge your paper inbox. When is the last time you've seen the bottom of your paper inbox at work and at home? Make it a goal this spring. Develop a paper management system to try to keep it that way.

☐ Eliminate e-mail clutter. Schedule some time to clear your e-mail inbox. Delete unnecessary e-mails, capture contact information, delegate tasks that can be done by someone else, send those "replies" finally, and set up filters and folders to avoid backlog in the future. Once you get your e-mail inbox down to one page (where you can see all e-mails without having to scroll down), try to maintain it.

☐ Go on a calendar diet. Take a look at your busy calendar and try to clear two or three social or work obligations that you said "yes" to that you now realize you should not have. We all do it (yes, even the professional organizer/time management expert!). Time is limited and precious; so think carefully about what you want to fill it with.

☐ Switch clothes. If you have not already done so, spring is the perfect time to switch your clothes from the cold weather items to the warm weather ones. Make four categories: Purge (damaged clothes), Donate (clothes that do not fit, you do not like, or that are out of style, but can be worn by those in need), Keep (clothes that fit, that you love and wear often), and Dry Cleaning/Tailoring (clothes that need to be dry cleaned or mended).

☐ Retire the Christmas decorations. You think I am kidding on this one? I am not. You know who you are. If the Christmas decorations are still up outside or inside your home, it is high time you put them away. Go do it, now. Your neighbors will thank you.

☐ Take care of your taxes. Yes, the official tax-filing deadline for personal income taxes is in April. However, many people take an extension, which means they will be filing later in the year. Stop procrastinating! Gather the documents to get those taxes done. And for those of you that have already filed, purge old tax records that no longer need to be saved (check with your accountant, but generally, the average person needs to maintain seven years of tax records in case of an audit claiming fraud). Don't forget to shred!

☐ Declutter the car. You will be passing many car washes held by various charities this time of year. You'd like to get your car cleaned, but you don't want anyone to see the inside! Sound familiar? Clear that car clutter. Empty out the garbage that has accumulated, bring in items that you purchased that are sitting in bags in the trunk, and return all sorts of "stuff" to its place in the home or office that found its way into your car. Ah, now go get that car washed or, better yet, treat yourself to a full car detailing.

- [ ] Organize outlying areas. Clear clutter in the garage and shed so that you can find the things you need this spring and summer. Take out the patio furniture and grill, dust off the bikes, and put away the snow blower. If you can't reach the lawn mower, chances are you will not use it as much. You may have put the Christmas decorations away, but with that jungle you call a yard, your neighbors will still not like you very much.

- [ ] Mend the medicine cabinet. Clear out any winter medications that you stockpiled, such as cough medicine and cough drops that have expired. Ditto for prescription medications that have expired. Buy yourself some new sunscreen, as that also has a limited shelf life.

- [ ] Makeup makeover. Makeup attracts bacteria. Therefore, purge any makeup that is "old." While there is no exact life span for makeup, if you haven't used it in a year, it is time to go. For more exacting makeup safety guidelines, do an online search on a reputable site.

- [ ] Overhaul your toothbrush. You should replace your toothbrush every three months. Period. Get a new one. It feels great!

Take your time, and work through this Spring Fling checklist. I guarantee you will feel a sense of renewal, while clearing the way for a productive and pleasant summer season.

Notes for spring cleaning:

Bon Voyage: Organized Travel Planning

I not only love to travel, I love to plan to travel. Therefore, it seems only fitting to share some of my well-honed travel planning tips so that you can enjoy an organized travel experience. The tips that follow may be common sense, but are not always commonly applied.

- **Create a personalized packing list**—Create a packing list on your computer so that you can revise it constantly as you travel and realize what you forgot and would have liked with you, and what you could have left behind. My packing list is organized into the following major categories: Essentials, For Business, For the Beach, For Overseas Travel, and For Active Vacations. It is then further broken down into subcategories that are specific enough to easily grab and check off each item without too much forethought. Make your list work for you and your family by personalizing it to match your needs. A vacation packing list template appears on page 125.

- **Freshen up your suitcases**—Air out your bags before you pack. There is nothing worse than putting clean clothes in a stale smelling bag. (Hint: A scented dryer sheet or lavender sachet can work wonders.)

- **Check luggage guidelines**—Go online and check your airline's luggage guidelines to ensure that your carry-on will fit, and that you will not be charged extra if you exceed the weight restriction for your checked baggage.

- **Pre-pack and weigh**—Print out your packing list in advance, and start laying out items so that you can get a visual snapshot of what you are bringing. Pre-pack your suitcase and weigh it. Better to make the cut at home when you can still remove things than to suffer an unexpected luggage fee at the airport.

- **Pack extra storage bags**—Pack a few storage bags for small items, like shoes. Make sure that one is waterproof in case you need to pack wet bathing suits on the trip back home.

- **Get your gadgets in order**—Empty memory cards and charge your phone and digital camera before you leave home. Consolidate power cords, chargers, and extra batteries in your carry-on.

- **Refill prescriptions**—Refill prescription medications in advance, and pack in your carry-on in their original packaging in order to pass muster with airport security. This also provides you with the prescription details in case the medication gets destroyed (melts in the sun, gets wet, etc.) or you are delayed and need to arrange a refill while still away from home.

- **Copy important documents**—Carry duplicates of your passport and visa (if traveling outside of the country), travel itinerary, and any other vital documents that you need for safe travel, and keep them in a different location than the originals while traveling. Consider also e-mailing electronic copies to yourself or storing at a secure online site.

- **Give your wallet a diet**—Pare down the contents of your wallet to only what you need during travel. Bring only essential documents, such as driver's license, medical insurance card (check to see if you have coverage if going outside of the country), passport, and credit cards.

- **Alert credit card companies**—Contact your bank and credit cards companies before you depart and inform them that you will be traveling, so that they will not be alarmed by out-of-town charges and put a security hold on your account.

- **Inventory the contents of your suitcase**—Take photos of your clothes, shoes, and jewelry, which will serve as documentation if your luggage gets lost or stolen. Download the shots onto your home computer or upload them to an online site just in case.

Now, you are prepared to travel. You can relax knowing that the essentials are in order. Enjoy, explore, and make great vacation memories. Bon voyage!

Notes for travel planning:

Master Vacation Packing List

Customize this template for your own travel purposes.

Clothes	Shoes	Toiletries	Medications	Things for the Journey	Miscellaneous
Sleepwear	Everyday shoes	Hair products	Vitamins	Passport	Tissues
Underwear	Sneakers	Hair accessories	Advil/Tylenol	Itinerary & tickets	Batteries
Socks/hose	Slippers	Blow dryer	Cold meds	Drinks	Flashlight
Pants	Sandals	Brush & comb	Allergy meds	Snacks	Umbrella
Shorts	Flip-flops	Soap	Prescription meds	Audio books	Toys for kids
Long-sleeved tops	Dressy shoes	Moisturizer	Digestive meds	Reading material	Jewelry & watches
T-shirts	Boots	Toothbrush & toothpaste		Maps	Laundry bag
Evening wear		Floss & mouthwash		GPS	Binoculars
Jackets		Eye care products		Music	
Bathing suit		Deodorant		Cell phone & charger	
Hats		Feminine hygiene		Camera & charger	
Winter accessories		Makeup		Money	
Exercise gear		Nail file, tweezers, scissors		Sunglasses	
Belts		Razor		Hand sanitizer	
		Sunscreen			
		Bug spray			

Back to School the Organized Way: Tips to Keep You and Your Child Organized All Year Long

It seems that the kids are going back to school earlier and earlier! Children often have mixed feelings at back to school time. Getting new backpacks, clothes, and school supplies can be fun, but the thought of returning to early mornings and nightly homework can bring on feelings of anxiety and stress.

Disorganization causes stress for kids, and can result in lack of concentration and lower level performance. Telltale signs of organizing problems in students are typically decreased participation in class, and the buildup of clutter (papers popping out of binders, backpack a mess, etc.).

The hardest age for organizing is generally middle school. Middle school aged kids think they are independent enough to handle everything, but usually are not. Also, they are starting to switch classes, which can be stressful and make it harder to stay organized.

Parents of school aged children often have stresses of their own, related to how they're going to stay organized with all of the paperwork that will soon be coming home from school. Preparing your home, family, and kids for back to school is of utmost importance. A little organization can make a big difference!

But how do you teach kids to be more organized? The goal is to encourage good habits that will last a lifetime—and practice a few techniques yourself.

General Back to School Organizing Tips:

- Create, maintain, and value organization in your home.
- Be creative in establishing organizing systems that appeal to different kids' learning styles.
- Establish routines to be maintained on a daily basis. Routines increase motivation and relieve stress.
- Involve kids in setting up and maintaining organizing systems. If kids are involved in setting up the systems, they feel invested in organizing and usually maintain the system more.

Set Up an Evening Routine

Prepare in advance

Most people are rushed in the morning, so the more you can do the evening before, the easier your mornings will be. Make lunches or hand out lunch money, choose clothing, gather homework, items for sports activities, library books, and permission slips and place in backpack, and charge cell phones before you go to bed. This way, the only things you have to handle in the morning are making the bed (if you even do that!), grooming, and eating.

Choose outfits in advance

If your kids have lots of energy before bedtime, have them spend a few minutes picking out their outfit for the next day, so there is no decision-making in the morning. If they are usually exhausted at night, consider spending some time on Sunday picking out the outfits for the week and hang them in their closet in the order of the days of the week. Then each night or morning, you can just pick out the appropriate hanger.

Work with your kids' natural schedule

Work with your kids' natural body clock if possible. If they have lots of energy at night, have them pack their backpacks for the next day and set them by the door before they go to bed. Or have them make their bed after school if they come home bounding with energy. If you work with their natural rhythms, you won't have a constant struggle on your hands.

Notes for the evening routine and schedule:

Set up a Morning Routine

Make Morning Checklists.

If your morning routine has fallen by the wayside during the summer, it is time to get back to a routine. Start waking the kids up a little earlier each day so their new schedule isn't shocking. Take a few minutes to make a master checklist for each child, listing each morning task and the time it should be done. A morning routine checklist can be as simple as:

> 7:00—Wake up.
> 7:05—Brush teeth and wash face.
> 7:15—Get dressed.
> 7:30—Eat breakfast.
> 7:50—Grab lunch and knapsack.
> 7:55—Walk to bus stop or get in parent's car and go!

You can utilize these types of checklists for after school and evening also. Older kids can have more advanced checklists that include completing homework, practicing a musical instrument, setting the table, putting out an outfit for the next day, etc. Update checklists as your kids develop new activities and goals.

Use Alarm Clocks.

Implement an alarm clock system for each child to help them get up in the morning. Yes, you may have to go wake them if they are very young, but eventually you want them to get up on their own.

Add Buffer Time.

Give yourself an extra 15 minutes each morning. If everything is done on time, then the kids can relax or read for 15 minutes, or eat breakfast more slowly!

Create a Lunch-Making Zone.

Create a lunch-making zone by storing everything you need to make lunch in a pantry or a kitchen cupboard or drawer. Store all of the lunch-making supplies in a convenient and easy to reach location with lunch boxes stored nearby. That way, you and the kids will have quick and easy access to everything needed to make lunch. When the kids are mature enough, they can make their own lunches by grabbing items assembly-style!

Notes for the morning routine and schedule:

Create a Home for Backpacks and Other School Items

Check boxes next to tips you intend to try, and shade in boxes when tips are implemented.

- [ ] Create a launching and landing pad. Have a place where school supplies and homework goes before it leaves the house. If shoes, backpacks, sports equipment, and other clutter have taken over the mudroom or your home's entry, you need a fresh start. Clean it out, then set it up to handle all the things kids will be bringing in and taking with them daily. Hooks for backpacks and bins for shoes and equipment will help make coming and going easier. Remind the kids to use the landing area when they arrive home from school, or ask each child to bring their backpacks directly to their homework station after school each day. This may require several reminders for the first month or so!

- [ ] Keep it simple. Be sure to set up storage systems where your children naturally gravitate. For example, if they enter the house through the garage, then set up hooks and shoe racks in the garage by the door. Don't expect kids to go all the way upstairs to their rooms to take off shoes and coats. Make it easy for them to succeed.

- [ ] Add hooks on the wall, Shaker style. Consider hanging some hooks in a foyer, mudroom, breakfast nook, kitchen, hallway, or the garage. Make sure the kids' school-related items are visible and accessible. You may not like the idea of having everything "out," but if it makes your morning routine run more smoothly, it is worth the sacrifice. Besides, you can get some really nice fashionable hooks these days!

- [ ] Set up homes for items. Help your kids succeed in finding what they need by giving their belongings a well-defined storage space. What types of homes should you set up?

  - Hooks your kids can reach for coats and backpacks.

  - Racks, baskets, or cubbies for shoes next to the door.

  - Baskets or plastic organizers with drawers for hats, scarves, and gloves.

  - A separate inbox for each child's homework.

  - A school supplies center to keep homework materials together such as pens, pencils, scissors, and glue.

- [ ] Don't forget the car and garage. The car and garage may seem like strange places to organize for school, but they often need a revamp before the new school year. Clear the clutter and start with a clean slate. And wouldn't it be nice to park the SUV or mini-van that you paid so much for in the actual garage?

Create a Study Area

Set Up a Homework Station.

If your children do not have specific areas to complete homework, consider setting up one or more homework stations. You may need to give up the dining room or kitchen table for a couple of hours each day, or you could try setting up a small desk and lamp in an unused nook in a quiet spot in your home. If your child is not using a computer to complete a school assignment, turn it off! Ditto with his or her phone!

A Desk Is Best.

Many kids wind up doing homework in the kitchen or dining room. Keep flat horizontal surfaces clear so kids can spread out and work at home. If children can fit a desk in their room, that is best as it avoids distractions. Keep the desk away from the play area if possible. Use the space you have well. If there is space for a desk for each child, use it! Think about creating the best learning environment.

Store School Supplies at their Point of Use.

Many kids do their homework at the kitchen table. So the kitchen is where you should store the extra school and craft supplies. You can use a kitchen cabinet. Not enough space in your kitchen? You can also store homework essentials in a small plastic caddy with a handle, allowing children to work anywhere in the house.

Use a Master Family Calendar

- An old-fashioned wall calendar stored on the refrigerator is a great organizing tool for most busy families. You can even consider color-coding based on person or activity. You should show young children the items on the calendar so they get the sense of the passage of time.

- Kids can start to keep their own calendar when they have activities to keep track of.

- For teens, consider an online calendar like Google Calendar for them and the entire family.

Learn Your Child's Organizing Style

Try to determine your child's primary learning style. The four learning styles are Visual, Auditory, Kinesthetic, and Tactile (see page 142). This will give you insight into his or her organizing style as well.

Many parents develop one system and apply it to everyone in the house equally. However, children have very different personalities and learning styles, so any new systems you establish should be customized, if possible, to each child. If your child's primary learning style is visual, for example, use visual cues such as labels and colors to reinforce learning.

Ask your child to offer his or her own suggestions. Involving your child in the process will hopefully make them more motivated to follow through as well.

Get the Right School Supplies for Your Child

Get Kids Involved.

Before you go shopping, shop at home, and take stock of what you already have. Take your children shopping for school supplies. Having your child participate in the process increases the chances that he or she will use the supplies!

Follow the Teacher's Rules.

Many teachers provide guidance as to what types of notebooks, folders, and binders the students should use. Speak to the teacher about what needs to be brought back and forth to school, what can be purged, what can be recycled, what can stay at home in files, etc. Regularly sort and purge! It makes it easier to keep up.

Choose the Right Tools.

- Binders—not everything needs to go in it!
- Use dividers in binders—that's what they're there for.
- Label books, binders, and backpacks.
- Simple expanding file (accordion) system to hold papers from school
- Color-coded files—one for each kid, or one for each subject
- Simple desktop file holder

The All-Important Backpack

- Your child's backpack is essentially his or her mobile office.

- Give your kid a say. Take your child with you to buy his or her backpack. Kids should have a say in choosing their own bag.

- Each day when your child gets home from school, the first thing he should do is deposit his backpack in the same spot and unpack necessary items.

- On a weekly basis, remind your child to take everything out of his or her bag, sort and purge it with your guidance, put away items that need to be stored long term at home, and repack items to go back to school.

Create a System for School Papers

Check boxes next to tips you intend to try, and shade in boxes when tips are implemented.

☐ Personalized Filing System. Kids should have their own personal file folders or paper storage system at home. Set it up in their room, using a system that makes the most sense to that child (portable open file holder, file drawer, accordion plastic holder, etc.). Name the files according to what your child calls each subject, and don't forget extra files for Certificates, Standardized Test Scores, Report Cards, etc., as well as creative topics like writing or poetry—whatever interests your child.

☐ Create a Shuttle File. Send your child to school every day with a special brightly colored hard plastic folder or small clipboard designated to only hold notes or instructions from the teacher. Guide your child to remove his or her shuttle file each evening and put it in your inbox, or his or her inbox, depending on which paper management system you are using. You can also guide your child to hang up shuttle file papers on a huge magnet on the fridge for you to see and act upon. This must be done first thing after school every day to be successful.

☐ Think Vertical. If you install shelving in kids' rooms, make sure to go vertical! It takes up less space and is visual. The desk can go below the shelving. Another great tool is a literature sorter, which looks like an old-fashioned mail slot system. The openings can be labeled for each subject just like a filing system would be. Wall pockets are also great ways to store papers in a kids' room without using a drawer.

Use a Memory Box for Each Child

As covered in detail in Chapter 3 (see pages 68–70), a Memory Box is a container in which each family member can store his or her most treasured possessions. The size should be big enough to fit the prized possessions, but small enough to grab and carry out of the house, in case of an emergency. The actual container can be a no-nonsense functional type, like a plastic bin, or it can be a lovely decorated stylish box, bin, or basket.

Start a Memory Box for your children's prized artwork, sentimental childhood possessions, schoolwork, etc. They can decide, with you, what goes in it. You can have a master Memory Box, and one for the current school year. At the end of the school year, your child, with your help, can revisit the year, purging any items that are not vital enough to go in the master Memory Box and selecting a few prized items to save.

Model Behavior for Your Children

- **Set a good example.** If you run around like crazy in the mornings looking for your keys, you are not modeling good organizing behavior for your kids. Set a good example by becoming better organized yourself! Work on your organizing challenges, as well as theirs.

- **Value organization.** Show that you strive for and value organization. If you value it, your children learn to do so too.

- **Communication is key.** Talk to your kids about how good organizational skills can improve all of your lives, and their performance at school. Remind them that the start of the school year is a great time to implement new systems.

- **Make it a habit.** Establish routines. Your child will become used to these daily habits, which will make them second nature and, therefore, easier to follow.

Notes for keeping kids organized:

Managing the Chaos of the Busy Holiday Season: A Survival Guide

Overwhelmed just thinking about the upcoming holiday season? Relax. If you take a little time to plan your holiday season, it will be more enjoyable for you and your family! Focus on practicing good organizational techniques and time management principles. Here are some tips to make the holidays enjoyable and the new year start off in a positive manner.

Setting Your Goals for the Holiday Season

We are pulled in so many different directions during the holidays: travel, family gatherings, parties and social events, shopping, baking, decorating, etc. Ask yourself: What do I want? This question is an invaluable guide for the holiday season. Think about what you want to do, as opposed to what you think others expect of you.

Decide on your goals for the holiday season. Do you want to spend quality time with family? Do you want to try your hand at hosting or baking? Or, do you want to relax and enjoy quiet time? Achieving your goals and creating a meaningful holiday season requires that you have smart plans in place, especially if you want to enjoy the season without overindulging or stressing out.

It is difficult to keep all of the mental clutter associated with the holidays in our head! Keep a "holiday central" notebook or create a memo in your handheld device. List items you want to do (notice I didn't say need to do!), gifts to be purchased, people to send cards to, etc. Create a holiday budget so you know what you want to spend and stick to it.

Dealing with Holiday Schedule Overload

All the things you want to do over the holiday season can create pressure if you don't bring your wants and needs into alignment and into a manageable schedule. Holiday joy comes from choosing the activities that are fulfilling for you. Avoid taking on too much at this time of year. If you're feeling too pressured, look for activities that you can reschedule until after the holidays, delegate, or say no to. Recognize that you can't do everything, especially if you want to enjoy your holiday season! Ask yourself: What is the worst thing that will happen if I don't do this?

Identify and avoid triggers. If going to certain events or seeing certain family members or friends stresses you out and always ruins your holiday experience, avoid that activity. If you must attend, shorten your visit. If you are watching what you eat, plan ahead by eating a small healthy meal at home, so you won't be as hungry at the event. Or plan out what you will eat at the event, allowing yourself a few treats that you only get to have once per year and stick to your plan.

If you regularly exercise, don't stop over the holidays! Carve out time for exercise, even if it is not as much time as you usually do. The holidays are stressful enough—don't miss out on a great form of natural stress relief!

Holiday Decorations

Pull out those holiday decorations (yes, all of them!). Take stock of what you will definitely use, and donate the rest in time for a family in need to use the decorations this season. Those decorations that are really just sentimental, but will never be used, should be stored in your Memory Box, not with holiday decorations.

Do you need to go all out with decorating this year? Maybe you want to scale back? Ask yourself if you still want to decorate as much as you used to, or are doing it out of habit or others' expectations of you. If so, then give yourself permission to keep it simple!

Holiday Cards

Buy your stamps in bulk or online. Check that you have current addresses for everyone on your holiday card list. If your contacts are stored on your computer, you can print labels.

Use a card sending service, such as Send Out Cards.

Consider sending New Year's or Valentine's Day cards instead. It's unique and can be an unexpected treat to the receiver!

Just don't do it! Don't send paper versions of holiday cards at all if you don't want to. Use e-mail and social media sites to send holiday wishes, or pick up the phone and call special people in your life.

Holiday Baking and Cooking

Prep your kitchen for holiday time. Purge any food items that your family is not eating (if they have not expired, donate to a nearby food pantry) and make a shopping list of what you will need for holiday cooking and baking. Choose recipes in your favorite cookbooks or online, and start making lists of holiday menus you want to prepare.

Plan out your baking and cooking time on your calendar as an appointment so you take it seriously and stick to it. Otherwise, you will find yourself cooking and baking at three o'clock in the morning the night before the occasion!

Gift Giving and Receiving

When gift giving, keep in mind that more isn't necessarily better—sometimes, it's just more!

Considering regifting. Yes, I said it! Look at gifts you have received and have not used yet, or gifts you bought and stored throughout the year. Consider sharing some of these gifts with those on your list if the gift is a good match. Don't feel guilty! It's the thought that counts, not how you came by it.

Think outside the box. Try to give gifts that won't just become clutter. Give perishables (make a favorite food item for a friend that always comments on your great cooking), gifts of experience (horseback riding for that niece that loves horses), gifts of time (babysitting for the couple that never gets to go out alone), etc. Be creative! Consider only giving gifts to children on your list, or deciding to donate to charities in people's names instead of buying presents. Just make sure to agree to do this with others on your list so you don't offend anyone come gift exchange time!

Ask people to be specific with what they want and need, and you do the same when writing out your wish list.

Let go of whatever gifts you receive that will just become clutter in your life, and do so without guilt! If you can't return it, donate it or give it to a friend that is likely to enjoy it.

The payoff to all of this planning? You won't have post-holiday regret syndrome! You'll be calmer and more available to enjoy the company of your family and friends, and you'll start the new year feeling empowered.

Notes for holiday organizing:

The Organized Job Search

Opportunity is missed by most people because it is dressed in over-alls and looks like work.

THOMAS EDISON

So, you are searching for a new job? Perhaps you are making a voluntary career transition. Maybe you have been laid off, or worse, fired. Regardless of the reason for your job search, one fact remains true: if you are conducting a job search, it is vital that you take an organized approach. Managing your job search is just like managing any other major project. You must create an infrastructure that allows you to operate in an efficient and productive manner. A successful job search requires forethought and action.

Tips for Conducting an Organized Job Search
Check boxes next to tips you intend to try, and shade in boxes when tips are implemented.

☐ Declutter and pre-purge. If you are embarking on a job search, it will be difficult to do so if your physical space is covered in clutter with piles of papers everywhere. Take some time to declutter. Purge any unnecessary items, file papers that you need to keep, recycle junk mail, and get some order back into that space! It will be easier for you to concentrate on your job search without all of that chaos and clutter around you. Just be careful that you don't spend too much time decluttering that you start using it as an excuse to procrastinate with regard to your job search. A few days should suffice.

☐ Create a job search schedule. Let's face it—searching for a job is hard work! If you are still employed while you are conducting your new job search, be prepared to have an extremely busy schedule. If you are currently unemployed, realize that you do, indeed, have a job—conducting a job search! Create a job search schedule that gives you ample time for all of the activities you need to focus on in order to succeed: résumé and cover letter preparation, surfing the Web for jobs, networking, interviewing, follow-up, etc. Block out time in your calendar for job search activities and treat that time as you would any traditional work commitment. Be consistent in the amount of time you spend each day and week on job search activities so that you keep your momentum going, and don't lose focus and miss valuable opportunities.

☐ Get your gear in order. Update your résumé, cover letter, references, and writing sample (if applicable). Ask for letters of recommendation and testimonials from previous or current supervisors, co-workers, and professional colleagues. Get some nice new stationery, and stock up on print cartridges for your printer. If you want to use an outside source for printing, some local printing shops will copy résumés for free during an economic downturn, so ask around! Be sure to have a computer with high-speed Internet access. An all-in-one machine for printing, copying, faxing, and scanning will also come in handy during a job search.

☐ Create a job search center. Set aside space at home (or wherever you will be conducting your job search activities) and make it job search central. Keep all of your job-search related supplies in that location, which will make it easy for you to find them when you need them. This will also help you to get into job search mode when you are in that space.

☐ Create a job search paper management system. You may be acquiring a lot of paper in your job search: resources, articles, sample résumés and cover letters, business cards of networking contacts, contact-us-later or rejection letters, etc. To the extent that you can maintain these items in a paperless fashion, go for it. But if you have to maintain hard copy paper, be sure to create a job search paper management or filing system, to be stored in your job search center. Keep it simple and use whatever system makes the most sense to you for ease of use (binder, portable filing bin, traditional filing cabinet, etc.).

☐ Plan job search activities. Plan out job search activities on a daily basis, such as phone calls to make, résumés to send, online applications to fill out, informational interviews to conduct, etc. Write down your job search activities as calendar items, to-dos, or tasks so that you take them seriously and treat them as measurable goals. Be realistic with regard to what you can reasonably accomplish in one day, but also challenge yourself!

☐ Track job search activities. Organizing your job search involves keeping track of all information and communications. Keep a record of where you sent your résumé and when, whom you have spoken to, when interviews took place, etc. This information will prove vital when deciding when to follow-up with leads. You can track all of this information using a calendar such as Outlook or Google, or an online job searching site. Whatever tools you use, it is important that you be able to track the status of your job search.

☐ Manage job search e-mail. In today's world, much of your job search will likely be conducted by e-mail. Therefore, before you even start your search, whittle down the amount of e-mail in your inbox so that you can hyper-focus on your job search e-mails, which will add up quickly. Create folders within your e-mail system using categories that make sense to you, such as Companies Applied To, Contacts Submitted Résumés To, etc. Also, if your personal e-mail address is inappropriate for a job search (suziesinglegal@gmail.com, for example), create a new e-mail address solely for the job search that is purely professional.

☐ Polish your online profiles. If you are conducting a job search in today's market, you would be remiss not to develop an online presence on social media sites, especially LinkedIn, which is the most professional of the social media sites and can essentially serve as your online résumé. But also consider other social media sites such as Facebook and Twitter. The opportunities are endless for employers and contacts to find you online. You may even have your own Web site, e-zine, or blog. Maybe you post articles on various article-marketing sites, or serve as a guest blogger on other blogs. If you maintain profiles on any social media sites, or have any type of online presence, be sure to polish your profiles so that they promote the image you want potential employers and contacts to see.

☐ Change your greetings. Change the message that greets callers for any phone number that you plan to use for your job search so that it sounds professional, and conveys the information you want callers to hear. Be prepared, not embarrassed!

☐ Stay positive. The longer a job search takes, the more chance you have of becoming negative about it. Try to maintain a positive attitude to the extent you can by monitoring your progress and staying active in your search. When the going gets rough during a job search, many people take a backseat and give up, which is counter-productive. Try to stay focused and make valuable contacts that are likely to lead to a job. However, don't be all consumed by your search for a job! Maintaining some balance in your life at this time will serve you well. Get adequate sleep, eat well, see family members and friends for pleasure, and make time for exercise.

Organization is one of the single most important things you can do to keep your job search manageable. Just like being organized helps you improve any other area of your life, home, or work, it will also help move along your job search in quick and efficient fashion and with less stress. It may even wind up being the key to finding that dream job you always wanted. Good luck!

Notes for an organized job search:

Organizing and Marriage—'Til Death (or Disorganization!) Do You Part

The goal in marriage is not to think alike, but to think together.
ROBERT C. DODDS

I've worked with many couples as a professional organizer. Many of them are married, some are domestic partners, others just roommates, etc. My background as a trained mediator often comes in handy during these client sessions. Often, during an organizing assessment, a client will mention that another user in the home cannot maintain an organizing system (or that the other user is the organizing problem!). When I inquire as to whether the system was created with the other user in mind, the client usually responds in the negative. Therein lies the problem.

Here is some insight into why couples often have a hard time agreeing on organizing systems, as well as some tips for getting and staying organized when faced with the challenge of a perceived "uncooperative partner."

Learn Each Other's Organizing Styles

Yes, everyone has an organizing style. Your organizing style usually matches your learning style. The four learning styles are Visual (learn by seeing), Auditory (learn by hearing/listening), Kinesthetic (learn by doing), and Tactile (learn by touching). Oftentimes, couples have very different organizing styles, making it difficult to set up and maintain shared organizing systems. Give some thought to the organizing style of each person using the system so that it makes sense to both users.

Reach Compromise on Shared Systems

If the organizing system you are creating is to be a shared system, you must give consideration to both users. Failing to consider both users is a common mistake and often causes the system to fall apart. So, do yourself and your partner a favor—communicate! Spend the time brainstorming how each person plans to use the system, and create a compromise that makes the most sense. The solution may be built around the most common user, or a combination of both users. This may take some extra effort, but usually results in a system that is maintained more effectively.

Tolerance for Clutter

Different people have different levels of tolerance for clutter. Some are "outies," meaning that they like the exposed areas like countertops, to be clear, but can tolerate clutter in hidden zones, like closets, drawers, closets, etc. They just want their outward appearance to look organized and they don't want to see the clutter. Others are "innies," meaning that the clutter can pile up on exposed surfaces, but their drawers, closets, and filing cabinets are pretty well organized. They are "pilers," leaving clutter out for all to see, but keep their private, inner spaces orderly. If an "innie" and an "outie" live together, there is often a big disconnect in the way they tolerate and handle clutter.

Leave Judgment Out

I know it's hard but you really need to make a conscious effort to approach your partner in a non-judgmental manner. Otherwise, your partner will just become defensive, and shut down to any creative solutions that could be reached. Try to approach your organizing projects with a sense of humor. If your partner has difficulty with setting up and maintaining organizing systems, realize that organizing is a skill and can be taught. Show some empathy and be patient as you try to find each other's organizing strengths and overcome weaknesses.

A Sanctuary of Disorganization

Just like Superman had a Fortress of Solitude, couples may need to allow each partner to have one space that is off-limits to the other partner's organizing efforts. It should not be a space that is shared, and probably not in the most public areas of the home. Allowing your partner to have one place where he or she can be him- or herself and not worry about you organizing it will go a long way to keeping you two from driving each other crazy. Think of it like granting your partner a "free pass" in that one area.

Notes for couples organizing:

Empty Nesters

When kids grow up and leave home, many parents suffer from "empty nest syndrome," which can result in depression, failure to move on, and turning the son or daughter's room into a shrine. From an organizing standpoint, if your grown-up child has permanently left home and no longer needs his or her room, consider it fair game! Go through the room with your adult child to determine what he or she will take, what can be donated, put in storage, or stored in your or his/her memory box. Then take that kid's former room and use it to your advantage. That is prime real estate.

The most common use of a former child's room is a home office. But you can also consider an exercise room, media room, craft/project room, etc. Be creative and turn it into something that fits your lifestyle now. It will not only boost the physical space in your home, but also will allow you to more easily accept the transition and embrace your new life as an empty nester.

Convert the Kid's Room

Now that your son or daughter has moved on, what could you use his or her former room for? Start visualizing how you could use the space in a way that matches your lifestyle and needs now.

Write your ideas here to motivate you to make the change!

Organizing After the Loss of a Loved One

I have worked with many clients over the years to organize after the loss of a loved one. Living in the greater New York metropolitan area, I helped many 9/11 widows and widowers organize after losing a loved one in the World Trade Center terrorist attacks. It is an emotionally draining process. My best advice is to take it slow and go at your own pace. After the death of a loved one, some people are tempted to sift through belongings and make decisions quickly. If this feels natural to you, fine. Consider checking with a grief counselor before moving too quickly through the process. But most people need more time after a loss to organize a loved one's possessions. So give yourself permission to grieve first, heal, and then organize later.

Take Your Time

Some clients needed only a few months, while others waited years until they took on the task of organizing their loved one's possessions. Indeed, some clients took on the project only due to necessity—moving, selling a house, clearing room for a new family member to move in, etc. If you aren't ready to handle the project but you must do so by necessity, then you may need to temporarily box up your loved one's possessions. Label the boxes to make it easier when you are ready to sort them at a later date.

Work with Others

Although many organizing projects can be done alone, some people find it helpful to work with another person to sort through a loved one's belongings after a loss. I also recommend doing the project in stages, as it can be emotionally and physically demanding. Be careful not to make decisions too quickly and be sure to check with other family members who may consider some belongings special that you are prepared to let go of. You may want to sort into categories based on family members, friends, donations to charity, antique appraiser/estate sale (for valuable pieces that you are not keeping), archive/storage, etc. I often tell my clients to choose items that embody the person's spirit, remind you of details of his or her personality, or carry special memories.

Be Selective

Remember that sometimes less is more. You don't want to be smothered by items that you don't have room for, or that will dredge up painful memories. You want to be able to enjoy the selected items and let them serve as reminders of your loved one's well-lived life.

Sadly, I lost my mother to cancer shortly after beginning to write this book. Many family members and friends assumed that I would quickly go in and sort my mother's belongings due to the fact that I am a professional organizer by trade. But I recognized that I needed time to process this profound loss, grieve, and heal before I could take on the task of going through her possessions. The only items that I took quick action on were the medications and medical supplies so that I could donate them before they expired and someone else could benefit from their use. I plan to take my time with the process, include family members, honor the possessions, and select items to keep and cherish. This way, my mother will always be with me.

I wish you warmth and strength if you are organizing after a loss. Be kind to yourself.

Exercise: Capturing Your Loved One's Spirit

Think of ten items that capture your loved one's spirit and gather them in one location. If they are not too large, consider putting them in a special container that you keep in a location that can be accessed easily. That way, you can take them out whenever you want to remember your loved one.

Notes for organizing after loss:

While seasonal changes, special situations, and life transitions can throw your routine organizing systems out of whack, you can get back on track. Using the knowledge you gained in this chapter, you will be better equipped to handle these special situations and transitions when they arise. Follow the guidelines above, take it one step at a time, and slowly find your way back to an organized life. It will be there waiting for you, and like a trusted friend, will welcome you back with open arms!

Notes

Courage is the power to let go of the familiar.

RAYMOND LINDQUIST

CHAPTER 7:
staying organized

Success seems to be connected with action. Successful people keep moving. They make mistakes, but they don't quit.

CONRAD HILTON

Congratulations! You made it this far. If you implemented many of the strategies included in this book, chances are you are seeing positive changes in your home, work, and life due to your newly-established organizing systems. Feels good, doesn't it? In fact, I bet you'd like to keep the systems going.

When you put in so much time and effort to get organized, the last thing you want is to backslide and wind up where you started. The good news is that you can stay organized once you reach an organized state of bliss. All that is required is active maintenance. Oh no, you think—more work! Yes, but remember, it is a lot easier to stay organized than it is to get organized.

Develop Simple Maintenance Routines

Integrate a daily and periodic maintenance program into your routine, but keep it simple.

Organizing is a way of life that requires maintenance and ongoing effort until it becomes second nature. Think about something you do every day, like brushing your teeth, for example. You don't need reminders, checklists, alarms, and prompts. Now imagine you just started brushing your teeth today. You may need a prompt to remind you to do this new activity. But eventually this new activity would become part of your routine and you would no longer need reminders. In order to stay organized, you need to slowly incorporate maintenance of organizing systems into your daily routines. After awhile, you don't even think about it anymore; you just naturally maintain your systems.

You've heard the old adage, "A place for everything and everything in its place." Well, it goes a long way if your goal is to maintain organizing systems. Put things away at the end of each day at home, and at the office. If you start something, complete it if possible. If not, put the project items off to the side so that they do not become clutter in your way. If you use up the last of an item in the house, replenish it. If you open something, close it. If you take something out to use it, put it away when you are done. Make this "finish it" policy a rule that all users of the organizing systems follow.

Fifteen Minutes a Day Keeps Clutter at Bay

Want to maintain an organizing system? Fifteen minutes a day keeps clutter at bay! Once you've created an organizing system that works, take 15 minutes a day to keep it that way. If it needs much longer than that, chances are it is too complex of a system, or you are still in backlog mode with too much clutter. If so, then you need to focus on continuing to declutter and setting up simple, user-friendly organizing systems.

It is entirely possible that some areas of your life will be in maintenance mode while others will still be in the process of getting organized. That is expected. While you are getting organized, you will naturally finish some areas before others. For the areas that are already organized, use your maintenance routines. For the rest, keep plugging away! You will get to maintenance mode if you hang in there, I promise.

Don't get caught up in the actual amount of time—15 minutes at work and 15 minutes at home is an average. Some people need much more time to maintain their organizing systems, some need much less. It depends how many organizing systems need to be maintained, how complex they are, how many users are involved, whether someone is sabotaging the system by not cooperating in maintenance efforts, etc. Use 15 minutes as a benchmark to measure your maintenance efforts.

Some people do their maintenance in the morning (washing dishes from last night's dinner, choosing outfits for the day, planning their schedule on their calendar, putting away files they are no longer working with, etc.), while others do it at the end of the day before they leave work and before they retire for the evening at home. The right time to maintain organizing systems is when it is easiest for you and you will actually do it. If you decide to maintain systems at the end of the day, be sure to finish activities at home and at work 15 minutes before you close shop, in order to leave enough time for maintenance. Remember, maintaining an organizing system should become second nature, like brushing your teeth every day. But it may take time for it to become a habit, so be patient. Meanwhile, 15 minutes a day will help keep clutter at bay, and maintain your orderly new life!

Don't Confuse Organization Maintenance with Housework

I often hear clients say that they spend hours maintaining organizing systems on a daily basis. When I ask them to describe their maintenance routine, they list housework and chores, such as food shopping, laundry, cooking, cleaning the bathrooms, and dusting the furniture. Those tasks are housework, not maintenance of an organizing system.

Maintenance of an organizing system at home may include putting toys away, getting your launching area ready for the morning, sorting the mail, hanging clothes back up that you tried on, etc. These types of organizing systems are the ones that you implemented to keep clutter from piling up and to streamline your home life. Housework and cleaning are necessary to maintaining a household but should not be grouped together with organizing systems. Housework and cleaning can take up to 20 hours per week. That is a lot more time than what is required to maintain organizing systems once they are set up, so don't confuse the two or you may get discouraged!

Strive for Progress, not Perfection

As with any behavior modification program (weight loss, smoking cessation, etc.), you should not strive for perfection. Why? Well, for one, perfection may be an unattainable goal, even for a certified professional organizer! Life is messy and unpredictable, made up of constant transitions and changes, all of which make it difficult to be perfectly organized at every moment. Strive for being well organized most of the time. Remember that being organized is the means to help you live a fruitful, high functioning, meaningful life. It is not the goal in and of itself.

In addition, perfectionism can cause a vicious cycle of behavior. If you set your organizing goals too high, you will most likely lose confidence when you fail to reach them. This lack of confidence may then cause you to give up and stop maintaining your organizing systems altogether. Don't get caught up in making the organizing systems perfect or you may get in your own way!

Constant Vigilance

You don't need to walk around with your organizing cap on at all times, incessantly obsessing over everything you do. But, you should periodically evaluate how your organizing systems are working. In order to maintain your organizing systems, you must keep up with changes in needs, goals, and priorities. As your life changes, so do your organizing systems. Systems can become outdated or obsolete. Evaluate your systems over time to ensure that they are still the best choices for you, and if not, start fresh by implementing new systems in their place.

If the system is still a good fit for you, but needs tweaking, then examine what needs to be done to bring it up to speed. Maybe you acquired too many items in the space and need to selectively declutter. If the space is finite (and so many really are—your closets, calendar, rooms in your home, etc. all can only hold so much), then be sure to implement some maintenance rules to keep the amount of items in check. Make adjustments for new items acquired, and purge old stuff that's become irrelevant. You can't just keep adding to your systems or they will eventually overflow.

Examine the Systems

Periodically examine your organizing systems. Are they working? Why or why not? Do any need tweaking? If so, schedule in time to rework those systems.

Make notes here of organizing systems that are no longer effective and how to improve them, then schedule time in your calendar to work on them.

System	Effectiveness	Strategies for Improvement
Time Management		
Home Organization		
Work Organization		
Paper, Bills, & Finances Organization		

Overcoming Lack of Motivation

What if you lack motivation to maintain your organizing systems? What if you are not in the mood, are tired, sick of the constant flow of possessions and paper in your home, workplace, and life? You need to focus on the end result, which is always an improvement over the current state. Continuing with the toothbrushing analogy, you sometimes need to just do it even when you are not in the mood, are rushed for time, or are tired. If you stop brushing your teeth, plaque will build up, causing gingivitis, and eventually your teeth will rot and fall out. Similarly, if you fail to maintain your organizing systems, clutter will build up, the systems will fail, you will become discouraged, and you will backslide. Then in order to get organized again, you will have to do double the work!

So, even if you lack motivation to maintain your organizing systems, remind yourself that maintenance is always easier than starting from scratch. Hopefully, the positive benefits you get from being organized will be more than enough to motivate you.

Notes for staying motivated:

Notes about my organizing journey:

You did it!

You've reached the end of the organizing journey. On this new path, you may notice many positive changes—more time and space, improved relationships, increased opportunities, financial savings, decreased stress, and better health. Don't lose sight of these positive benefits of being organized. They will inspire you to continue down the path of being organized for a long time to come.

However, if you ever find yourself straying from the path of being organized, realize that you can get back on course. If you need a refresher at any time, just pick up this book and go to the section that you need help with, or read it all the way through again. Like an old friend, it will welcome you back with open arms, and leave judgment aside.

Now go forth and live the organized life you were meant to live.

Notes

You make the world a better place by making yourself a better person.

SCOTT SORRELL

About the Author

Photo by Diane Pell

Lisa Montanaro is a Certified Professional Organizer, a business and life coach, and a motivational speaker. Drawing upon her experience as an attorney, mediator, teacher, and performer, Lisa founded LM Organizing Solutions, LLC in 2002 and has helped hundreds of people live better lives and manage more productive companies and organizations. Lisa is a member of the National Association of Professional Organizers (NAPO) and the National Speakers Association (NSA). She has presented professionally to audiences throughout the United States, has been interviewed by television and radio hosts, and is a frequent guest expert for teleclasses and webinars. Lisa's work has been featured in the media, and her written content has been widely published online and in print. She lives in Warwick, New York, with her husband, Sean, and their two dogs, Dublin and Jerry. Find more information about Lisa at her Web site, **www.LMOrganizingSolutions.com**, and blog, **www.DecideToBeOrganized.com**.